Downshift
to the
good life

one good idea can change your life...

Downshift to the good life

Scale it down and live it up

Lynn Huggins-Cooper

CAREFUL NOW

We hope we've provided you with some great ideas on how to make your life more relaxed, self-sufficient and healthy. We sympathise with the stress and frustration you feel in your current life and would love you to regain your *joie de vivre*. While we wish you every luck in your future endeavours we feel that it's only right for us to point out that we can't be there to pick up the pieces if the neighbours don't like you turning your suburban garden into a miniature farm, your country idyll turns out to be a money pit or you and the chickens just don't get on. It's your life so get out there and take control of it.

Copyright © The Infinite Ideas Company Limited, 2005

The right of Lynn Huggins-Cooper to be identified as the author of this book has been asserted in accordance with the Copyright, Designs and Patents Act 1988.

First published in 2005 by
The Infinite Ideas Company Limited
36 St Giles
Oxford
OX1 3LD
United Kingdom
www.infideas.com

A CIP catalogue record for this book is available from the British Library.

ISBN 1-904902-37-5

Brand and product names are trademarks or registered trademarks of their respective owners.

Designed and typeset by Baseline Arts Ltd, Oxford
Printed by TJ International, Cornwall

Brilliant ideas

Brilliant features

Each chapter of this book is designed to provide you with an inspirational idea that you can read quickly and put into practice straight away.

Throughout you'll find four features that will help you to get right to the heart of the idea:

■ *Here's an idea for you* Take it on board and give it a go – right here, right now. Get an idea of how well you're doing so far.

■ *Try another idea* If this idea looks like a life-changer then there's no time to lose. *Try another idea* will point you straight to a related tip to enhance and expand on the first.

■ *Defining idea* Words of wisdom from masters and mistresses of the art, plus some interesting hangers-on.

■ *How did it go?* If at first you do succeed, try to hide your amazement. If, on the other hand, you don't, then this is where you'll find a Q and A that highlights common problems and how to get over them.

Introduction

Flashback: eighteen years ago, I proudly bundled up my newborn in fluffy white blankets, popped him in the pram and set off up Barking Road. Ten minutes later he was covered in specks of black dirt and my quest to move to the country had begun.

Two years later, we moved to a small village in County Durham where we happily and quickly became part of the community. Fast forward seven years and we moved to my dream home – a rambling sandstone farmhouse with 14 acres. The first morning I woke up in my new house, with sunlight flooding through the window at the end of the bed and sheep bleating on the hillside, I cannot describe the feeling of well-being that flooded through me. I felt as though I was on holiday for the first few weeks as I wandered around *my* fields and sat in a happy heap on springy grass, with butterflies and wildflowers all around me.

As you may have guessed from all this gushing, I'm something of a downshifting evangelist. I grew up with my hands in the soil; in my earliest memories I am playing on my parents' allotment. My mother's kitchen was always full of home grown produce – gluts of crunchy green beans, sweet cherry tomatoes bursting with flavour, and heaps of raspberries that stained our fingers red. At my father's knee I learned about making 'muck tea' with a bag of manure suspended in an old bath of rainwater; I chased toads under the compost heap and learned to turn the steaming pile for my trouble. They still have the allotments as pensioners, today – and continue to win prizes. Growing my own food is in my blood.

There is something amazing about wondering what to make for dinner, deciding you want cauliflower cheese, then going out into the garden to cut the fresh cauliflower and the herbs to make it. And gathering eggs from your own hens is sublime. Even shop-bought free-range eggs don't come close to an egg that's hot from the hen's bot! We can even pick wild food in our own fields and hedges, content in the knowledge that they are free from pesticides and other chemical nasties. These experiences are priceless – for us and for our children.

The benefits in downshifting for children are immense. They learn where food comes from, for starters. A recent MORI poll commissioned by the National Farmers' Union in the UK made disturbing reading. Almost half of the children aged between eight and eleven surveyed believed margarine comes from cows. A quarter of the children thought bread was made from potatoes or rice. Half of the children did not know ham comes from pigs. These children live in a sanitised, vacuum packed world where pre-prepared food is bought from a multinational supermarket and 'assembled' at dinnertime.

When they help to plant, water, weed and nurture the vegetable patch, children have an immense sense of achievement. Picking baskets of fruit (my kids are far more of a danger to my strawberries and raspberries than any bird or slug) and bringing them into the kitchen to make fragrant jam is the sort of memory that can't be beaten. The excitement generated by gathering fresh eggs has to be seen to be believed (and that's me as well as the children).

My children also benefit from having me around. I'm here as they go to school in the morning and I'm available when they come home at night. I work from home, writing at my computer in front of a window that looks out over one of my fields. I often get to watch wildlife as I work.

Today I can see the frame of my exciting fortieth birthday present from my husband. No bottles of perfume or sparkly gems this year; I got my heart's desire – a huge polytunnel. I can't wait to fill it with propagating plants and tender fruit and vegetables. I know putting the cover on will be a major task, but a group of us will manage it together. That sums up one of the mainstays of my view of downshifting: we become more self-reliant in many ways, but in others we learn how interconnected we are with those who share our vision. That is not just locally, with friends and neighbours, or in smallholding or gardening groups; it can even be through online groups and lists, where a vast reservoir of experience and knowledge, gladly shared, awaits. The best people to share problems and successes with are those who have been there, done that. That is where the prospective downshifter should begin.

Find out as much as you can before you get started. A daydream of living and working in the country is a great thing, but reality can be harsh. Be prepared for long hours, and dirty and physically demanding work. If you decide to go down the smallholder route, you are close to nature and she is capricious. Last week, gales flattened my new wooden outbuilding. I will rebuild it with stronger anchoring. Frost comes along and pokes icy fingers into rashly sprouting plants and blasts them black. So you replant, and use cloches. Hens decide to stop laying once it gets cold, but they still need feeding and cleaning out.

To be a successful smallholder, you have to be awkward and a bad (if at times sanguine) loser. You have to be prepared to fight to keep going – and to love your land passionately. If you are downshifting to the country on a whim – don't. Visit for holidays. But if you hanker after food fresh from the earth, and are prepared to work for it, there is nothing better.

Congratulations. You're thinking hard enough about downshifting to buy this book. I have written it to share my experiences of downshifting – good and bad – with you. Whether you decide to put *some* or *all* of the ideas in this book into practice is up to you – but whatever you choose will enhance your life.

1

Reality check

Live to work – or work to live? Think carefully about your work/life balance or you may find yourself churning round the work treadmill so intensely that life passes you by completely.

You work late, arriving home just in time to see your children as they go to bed if you're lucky. You eat, do household chores, and go to bed. In the morning, you get up and start all over again. Surely there must be a better way to live.

Do you feel that you are struggling to find meaning in your life? Feel as though you're in a spiritual and emotional vacuum; or that you're dislocated from anything 'real'? Perhaps you try to fill the void with 'things'. You go on recreational shopping trips for new, meaningless trinkets until you are trapped by an ever-growing pile of *stuff*. It may be attractive, and no doubt it's expensive, but it conspires to weigh you down. Acquiring more stuff becomes an obsession – or an addiction. Each boost gives you a high, but it is fleeting and soon needs replenishing.

Here's an idea for you...

If you're thinking of downshifting, make a list of the pros and cons. This might sound like the old-fashioned advice your mum used to give you, but it works. Dare to daydream. Create the picture of how you want your life to be. Once you have this in your mind, craft your list of pros – more time with the children, less stress, no commuting, being more self-sufficient. But consider the cons too. Will you be able to cope with isolation, hard work, harsh weather and surviving on a reduced income? Read as many personal accounts of downshifting as possible so you get a realistic picture of the bliss – and agony – you may experience.

TOO MUCH STUFF – NOT ENOUGH TIME!

You gather wealth and possessions to gain kudos. The amount of expensive *stuff* we have is a measure of our success. But there's a nagging feeling in the back of your mind: although you are resources rich, you are time poor. You spend your money on buying back time – paying other people to care for your children, clean your home, do your ironing. Your mind races constantly, so you pay for relaxation and exercise – going to the spa, the gym and the beauty therapist.

Increasing numbers of people are now refusing to be a part of this 'stress and spend' lifestyle. In Europe alone, 12 million people have decided to downshift. That may mean moving to a less stressful – and potentially lower income – job and moving to a smaller, less expensive house. At the other end of the scale it may mean moving to a smallholding in the country and living a more self-sufficient lifestyle. Whatever form of downshifting you decide to experience, you must ensure you are fully prepared for a major lifestyle change.

You may be excited by the idea of living a more simple life and working for yourself, either setting up your own business or you may fancy freelance work for other companies. You may also yearn to spend more time outdoors, with your hands in the soil growing your own food and collecting eggs from your warm, fluffy chickens.

Do you want to tackle the 'stuff' you are accumulating and have a clear-out? Have a look at IDEA 7, *Cut the crap: decluttering for dummies*.

Try another idea...

LOOK BEFORE YOU LEAP

What you don't want to do is leap in, feet first, and have to crawl ignominiously back to city life in a year's time – as many people do. They did the dreaming, but forgot to take a cold, hard look at the challenges they would face. Can you face the isolation – either the type that can come with rural life, or the type that can come with working from home? If you hope to spend lots of time outside, are you prepared for bitter cold? It's not always sunny and idyllic, you know.

Your baseline at all times should be the answer to this question: what gives you joy? Then take steps to include it in your life.

'Downshifting isn't just about getting away from what you don't want, it's also about moving towards what you really want to do.'
NICK WILLIAMS, author of *The Work We Were Born To Do*

Defining idea...

3

How did
it go?

Q **I've always fancied living on a smallholding, but the more I read, the more scared I get about the amount of gruelling, messy work involved. Do these reservations mean my dream will wither and never come true?**

A *It's wise to be cautious. I've lost count of the bitterly cold days when I've dreaded the chores facing me. But I wouldn't swap my life for anything – organic veggies on my doorstep and startled deer staring at me as the mist clears in the early morning. The key is to check out what you can cope with. Stay on a smallholding for a break and see what work is involved. Read, read, and read some more – books, websites, online communities – to get as full and real a picture as possible. You may still want a smallholding or you could decide to compromise and move to a more rural area with a large garden for vegetables and a few hens. Just make sure you make the right choice for you and your dream will blossom.*

Q **Can you really live a self-sufficient life without moving to the country, like that show on TV? I'd like to downshift, but I don't really want to move away from my house in the suburbs.**

A *Although the TV programme was played for laughs, it is possible to downshift to an extent without moving. For example, look at your outgoings – where can you make savings that will enable you to work fewer hours? How large is your garden? You can grow a wide variety of crops in an amazingly small space. Do your homework and you should be able to make real changes in your situation.*

2

Commuting costs

Commuting has costs in terms of money, time, and the environment – but perhaps most importantly in terms of personal stress. There are alternatives that offer benefits to you, and your employer.

Outside major cities, which often have well-developed mass transit systems, an average of 70% people commute to work by car, so gridlock in urban areas is inevitable. This, of course, results in stress and frustration — before the working day even begins!

THE COSTS OF COMMUTING: *FINANCIAL*

Given that employees pay £13 billion to commute 3,000 miles per year by car in the UK alone, it's mind-boggling to imagine what the expense might be across the whole world. Even workers who use public transport can find the costs of season tickets punitive. Businesses also pay a price in terms of mileage allowances, congestion charges and lost time as employees travel a further 1,600 miles for work purposes.

Think about going part time at work if it's financially possible, and spend the released time building up freelance work or your own home business. This will initially be hard work, but it will ease the path towards downshifting in the long run. Rather than going 'cold turkey', which can be a major risk, dip your toes in the water and see if you can find alternative ways to make money. I began to write when I was still teaching full time. Then I worked as a supply teacher and a sessional lecturer while I built up my writing career. My 'commute' today is to fall out of bed, tumble down the stairs, grab a coffee – and the day begins!

THE COSTS OF COMMUTING: *ENVIRONMENTAL*

In the mid-1970s, transport accounted for one fifth of the energy consumed in the developed nations. It now uses up one third and traffic accounts for roughly 25% of carbon dioxide emissions. This pollution can lead to health problems, especially in urban areas where air quality may be poor. Traffic also creates noise pollution, which is a significant factor in stress levels for local residents.

Major road building programmes – supposedly to decrease road congestion – affect the environment. New schemes are threatening countless sites of special scientific interest (SSSIs).

Commuting even turns semi-rural villages into 'dormitories' because the people leave in the morning and don't return until nightfall. This has implications for vital local businesses, such as shops and post offices, which may eventually be forced to close because of the lack of day-to-day customers. Looking round our nearest village during the day, you could be forgiven for thinking that a smart bomb had eradicated the five to sixty age group entirely, leaving a population of retirees and rugrats.

THE COSTS OF COMMUTING: *HEALTH*

You'll be thoroughly unsurprised to hear that commuting causes stress! Sitting in heavy traffic worrying about being late for meetings makes your stomach churn and your chest tighten. You are more likely to react aggressively to any incidents that occur. Long, busy or difficult journeys can make you feel fatigued and drained even before you reach work. Train journeys can be just as stressful as driving when trains are late, delayed or crammed with commuters. Almost half of people say that rush hour commuting is the most stressful part of their day.

The air pollution caused by all those commuting cars has been implicated in the rise in cases of asthma. The pollutants are generous: they do not just fall outside the car, covering passers by in a layer of grime, they also affect the driver inside the car. Quite apart from asthma making you feel wretched, there is a monetary cost. This obviously is felt by the health services, but it also has implications for employers. The number of working days lost due to asthma doubled in the decade between 1982 and 1992.

Fancy cutting out the commute by working full time from home? Check out IDEA 9, *Happy homebody*.

Try another idea…

'*Never doubt that a small group of thoughtful, committed citizens can change the world. Indeed, it is the only thing that ever has.*'
MARGARET MEAD, US anthropologist

Defining idea…

WHAT'S THE SOLUTION?

Quite simply, less commuting. Our work culture needs to change to allow more flexible working – not just so that people commute at different times of day, because that is only shifting the problem. Greater provision for working from home would improve matters all round, and the technology is available already. Laptop computers, virtually universal availability of broadband internet access and the gradual introduction of videoconferencing is making it easier for people to spend at least some of their working life at home, leaving 'office time' for *necessary* face-to-face meetings.

These arrangements would improve life for employees. It would also have knock-on benefits for companies: a less stressed workforce means potentially fewer working days lost to sickness and lower staff turnover.

Q **I'm nervous about working remotely. My office has a real adrenaline-driven, full-on work ethic. People are respected for arriving early and leaving late. Will colleagues take me seriously if I work from home some of the time? Will they even believe I am working?**

How did it go?

A *The bottom line has to be do you want to work in that atmosphere? Give the idea a try and see how it goes. You may find that you take the lead in changing the culture in your workplace. If things become too difficult, or you feel marginalized, it may be necessary to take more dramatic steps and change your job for a more flexible arrangement.*

Q **How can I stay in the job I have now but maximise my personal time? I want to downshift, but it has to be 'baby steps'!**

A *Negotiate to make your working week as flexible as possible. Could you work fewer hours, or even part time? Could you work four nine-hour days instead of five shorter days? Could you work different hours to reduce your travelling time? Talk to your boss.*

9

3

All aboard?

You've decided to downshift. You're brimming with enthusiasm, but who's that in the corner with a face like thunder? Make sure the family shares your dreams before you go too far!

It's all very well daydreaming about your downshifted Shangri-la but without your family's agreement and support you may as well stop now because it won't come to pass.

Downshifting is a major, life-changing event. If you have a partner and/or children, they must share your dream or you are doomed to fail. Major lifestyle changes are stressful, and you will need support. If your partner is coerced into moving to a smallholding in the country and his or her natural habitat is a swanky wine bar or Harvey Nicks, you will both regret it.

With your partner on board, you're more than half way there because you will have someone to share the challenges – and there *will* be challenges – as well as the triumphs. If he or she is ambivalent, you have a serious PR job on your hands. It may help if you point out the reasons you need to downshift. Talk about the way in

Here's an idea for you... **Before you sit down to have 'the talk' with your partner, prepare as though you are going to a business meeting – think things through carefully, do your homework and prepare your arguments. Talk reasonably about your ideas – hard when you are feeling passionate, but necessary! Calculate the minimum you will need to live on in your new life, and explain how you will meet those costs. Explore different ways of earning an income, perhaps by working as a freelance. You need a safety net, and you need savings. Ideally, you should set aside enough money to keep you for six months before you begin.**

which your day-to-day work adversely dominates your life. The technology that makes your work easier can make your life harder, for example: you are available almost twenty-four hours a day, via e-mail, mobile phone and instant messaging. It's hard to leave the office behind when you take the technology home.

Talk about what work is doing to the pair of you. Are you healthy? Or are you victims to one illness after another? Do you feel constantly tired? That may mean you are overworking, or it may mean you are becoming depressed by the circumstances of your life. Do you drink too much? Alcohol is often used as a quick fix to relax after a 'hard day', and that easily turns into a habit. Do you regularly skip meals because you are too busy? Or do you 'comfort eat' to crush down the feelings of stress and powerlessness that modern working conditions create?

You may have found that your personal relationships have all become work centred, so even social occasions are bogged down by discussions about office matters. Your partner may feel that your work dominates your life to the point at which downshifting becomes not just desirable, but necessary. Make no mistake, if you downshift – particularly to live on a smallholding – you will still be incredibly busy. The work is hard, takes many hours and like any other form of work it expands to fit the time available. But although you will not have more time, the time you do have can be much more flexible. You will be able to spend more time working side by side with your partner, working towards a common goal, which can be very cementing for your relationship. You will also be able to be flexible about childcare, sharing the labour more equally, and spending more time with your children.

Worried about how your kids will react to moving to the country? Read IDEA 17, *Cabin fever families: downshifting with children.*

Try another idea...

I have found that when I spend more time with my hands in the soil, it's like I am literally *grounding* myself. I become less short-tempered and more nurturing. Without going 'New Age' on you now – just when you were listening – I've discovered that I need that contact with the natural world to function properly. The irony is, after making the momentous decision to give up work outside the home and write full time, I have found myself busier than ever. It is too easy to get into a spiral: if I take on that contract, I can buy a greenhouse; if I take on that project, I can buy more goats; if I write that book, it will pay for that building work. I end up working longer hours than I did before I left the rat race. Guard against losing sight of your aims and being seduced back onto the treadmill.

'Change. It has the power to uplift, to heal, to stimulate, surprise, open new doors, bring fresh experience and create excitement in life. Certainly it is worth the risk.'
LEO BUSCAGLIA, Lecturer and counsellor

Defining idea...

13

How did it go?

Q   Is it really possible to freelance from home? Or is being far from the city the kiss of death work-wise?

A   *It all depends what you do. I 'telecommute' to work. My publishers are virtually all hundreds of miles away. Apart from a couple of trips annually to their offices, I work from my study at home. God bless the internet! Do you have skills you can use in this way? Do you have skills that mean you can work on temporary contracts – such as supply teaching, photography, accountancy, training and consultancy?*

Q   My partner is a bit worried that our children will be missing things if we move to the country. How can I put her mind at rest?

A   *Talk about the benefits: having you around more, less pollution and traffic, and the space and freedom to discover their own place in the world. There are schools, clubs and sports facilities in the country too. And you can always visit the nearest town a couple of times a month for the theatre or cinema. Realistically speaking, how often do you go now while it's on your doorstep?*

4

Cheap as chips

Frugal living – is it Scrooge-like penny pinching or everyday money saving? Well, it's up to you to decide how far you want to go.

It's actually possible to save a lot of money around the house in very easy ways. That money soon adds up — and the more you save, the sooner you'll have financial freedom.

Household cleaning is one area where savings can be made. The basic thing to remember is *don't believe the hype!* Instead of using the latest expensively advertised 'miracle' cleaning fluid, consider using old-fashioned, cheap and effective home-made cleaners. The three best materials to buy for a variety of cleaning jobs around the house are white vinegar, bicarbonate of soda and your favourite scented essential oil. Those, combined with hot water and a bit of good honest elbow grease, will tackle most jobs – and with no nasty chemicals so it's environmentally friendly as well as very cheap.

A teaspoon of bicarbonate of soda on a damp cloth gets rid of most of the stains that proprietary cream cleansers do. A teaspoon can also be added to a white wash to make it bright. A large box of bicarbonate of soda can be bought cheaply at the chemist's or hardware shop.

It is worth shopping around for the cheapest electricity, gas, and other suppliers – customer loyalty doesn't necessarily pay. There are websites that allow you to compare prices, such as uSwitch.com in the UK and upmystreet.com in the USA. Make sure you find the best deals before you contact a variety of irritating sales people who might never leave you alone, ever – not even when you're dead!

Add a few drops of essential oils, like lavender or chamomile, to water in a washed out spray bottle (ask friends to save these for you; they're very useful). This can be used lightly when wet dusting, which is good for getting rid of dust mites that can cause allergic reactions. It makes the room smell great, too! Tea tree oil can be used as an antibacterial cleaner in this way too.

White wine vinegar is a great surface cleaner for glass – TVs, windows, glass doors, mirrors, etc. Fill a washed out spray bottle with half vinegar and half water and use sparingly. A crumpled up newspaper is a great 'polishing cloth' to finish these surfaces. When you finish with it, shred it and add it to the compost heap. Vinegar is also great for getting rid of limescale (simple chemistry if you think about it; limescale is *lime*scale, so it is alkaline, and vinegar is acid).

Instead of carpet cleaner, vacuum thoroughly to raise the nap and then sprinkle baking soda on the carpet. Leave overnight, then vacuum again. This removes smoke, pet and food smells.

A great way to clean aluminium cookware and utensils is to use cream of tartar. Fill the pan you want to clean with water and add cream of tartar (two teaspoons per litre). You can put aluminium utensils inside the pan. Bring it to the boil and simmer for a while until the pan looks clean, then rinse.

I've never seen the point in spraying chemicals around the room to make it smell better. I actually think that all it does is make it smell *different*. Don't forget in these days of double glazing that an open window will ventilate and freshen a room. To make a natural air freshener for the kitchen, pop a few cloves and a cinnamon stick in water and simmer them until the kitchen is full of the smell – this is a good one if you are selling your house, too, because it is a 'homely' smell.

Worried about making your money go the distance? Consult IDEA 5, *Check out your assets*.

Try another idea...

When utility bills arrive, it seems as though you are paying money for nothing. You know you run the washer, lights, TV, computers etc., but can it really cost that much? Well, the short answer is *yes*. You need to find savings.

Install energy saving light bulbs all over the house. They are more expensive, but last longer and save money in the long run. It goes without saying that you should switch off lights when you leave a room.

Make sure you switch off all of your electrical appliances at the wall before you go to bed. Apart from minimising the fire risk, lots of electrical appliances use a surprising amount of power even when they are on standby.

At the risk of sounding like your granny, I would urge you to peg washing outside to dry. It saves power if you don't use the tumble dryer, and the sunlight can help to brighten whites. Alternatively, use an indoor airer.

'Our life is frittered away by detail... Simplify, simplify.'
THOREAU

Defining idea...

How did it go?

Q **My mother is always going on about 'batch cooking' to save time and power. Does it work?**

A *Actually, mother* does *know best in this case! When you use your oven make sure it's full. Batch cook food, such as lasagne or hotpot, and freeze the extras. That saves you time by having a home-made 'ready meal' in the freezer, and it saves power; not only cooking power, but freezer power too. This is because an empty freezer wastes money. Fill it up with double batch cooking or with reduced-to-clear goods, which cost next to nothing.*

Q **At the risk of sounding anal, I have examined my supermarket till receipts for the past two months to see how I can save money. One of the things that costs me a ridiculous amount of money is washing powder. I usually buy the same branded powder every time because I know it works. Is it worth trying own brand stuff? Surely you get what you pay for.**

A *Not necessarily; you may just be paying for the advertising. Get past your brand name snobbery and buy generics. Own brand washing powder can be great – or dismal. Try a few until you find one you like. Watch out for special offers like 'buy one, get one free' and stock up.*

5

Check out your assets

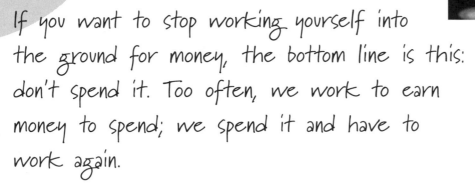

Controlling your money gives you control of your life. It buys your freedom. Money under control gives you a breather and can release you from a job you hate.

If you want to stop working yourself into the ground for money, the bottom line is this: don't spend it. Too often, we work to earn money to spend; we spend it and have to work again.

With a financial cushion, you can choose to work part time or take a risk and start a business. You tie yourself to a stressful, unsatisfying job by continually living beyond your means. You live from pay cheque to pay cheque, saving nothing.

WHAT CAN YOU DO?

Break down how much you spend each month. You could be in for a surprise. It certainly was for me when I carried out this exercise! I found I was buying myself little 'treats' to cheer myself up because I was so tired, and I was getting down about working so hard. What I couldn't see until then was that the 'treats' I was

Here's an idea for you...

Track your spending for a week. Be really anal and write down *everything* you spend, even including a cup of coffee. It's tedious and seems small minded, but it gives you an idea of where your money is going – and that could be a real wake up call.

buying were getting more expensive as my income rose. That meant I was forced to work harder to afford the treats – so I worked harder. The upward spending spiral needed to be broken, and tracking my spending was one way to do that. Today, there are still many treats and rewards in my life. They might involve giving myself time to dig a new veggie bed (therapeutic, trust me), or they might involve a splurge on a meal out. I just make sure that I no longer live beyond my means.

It may be a nasty shock when you identify where you spend your money, but it's better than going on complaining that you don't know where your money goes. Do you spend a lot on takeaways because you come in late and tired? Do you spend a lot on ready meals because you have no time to cook? Are there things you are spending money on that you can do without? Don't get into the mind-set that it's about denying yourself – instead, think that it's about making choices to bring you towards a positive goal, such as working fewer hours.

CREATE A FINANCIAL PLAN

Once you have a real picture of where your money goes, make a list of expenses such as your mortgage or rent, utilities, etc. Are there any ways to economise there? For instance, using energy saving bulbs and appliances can save money, as well as the environment. Then look at monthly bills such as satellite TV, club membership, etc. Is there anything you are willing to give up to move you towards being able to work fewer hours or to retire earlier?

If you want to earn a little more, get some pointers from IDEA 8, *Supplementing is great for your health.*

Try another idea...

Use any money you can gather from the savings and cut-backs you choose to make to pay off consumer debt. This is even more important than saving. Credit and store cards charge ridiculously high interest rates and should be paid off as soon as possible. Really think hard about whether it is worth buying anything on credit. That cute little piece of plastic does more than anything else to keep you on the work treadmill. Look at any debts you have closely. Prioritise them, paying off those with the highest rates of interest first. If you have credit card debt, shop around for a new card with a 0% offer on balance transfers. This can give you months of payments that hack lumps off the debt rather than merely pay off interest charges. Pay as much as you can every month. Once you are out of debt, think about saving. It is worth talking to a financial advisor at this point to find a savings plan that fits your needs.

These financial plans may mean that you can't buy everything you want. But, think carefully: what do you want more – consumer goods or the financial freedom to work less and enjoy life more?

'To know when you have enough is to be rich.'
LAO TZU

Defining idea...

21

Q   **I have to have expensive clothes for my highly paid job – there are certain expectations, and without the sharp suits I will not be taken seriously. How can I *possibly* cut back?**

A   *Work out just how much money you spend on high-status clothes and grooming simply to create a persona. Are you spending huge amounts and working hard to maintain an image that isn't really you? If you're spending so much time and money to keep up appearances, are you finding time to develop yourself? Do you ever stop to think about who you really are, what makes you happy, and what is important to you? It sounds as though the expectations of the job have you in a straitjacket. It may be that you are ready to make changes to your career.*

Q   **It sounds as though you want me to give up everything I enjoy! Do I have to do that to downshift?**

A   *No one is saying you have to do without treats to downshift. The key aim of downshifting for me is having the time to do what brings me joy. If eating in good restaurants brings me joy I budget that into my spending to make sure it happens. There will be pleasures you will be willing to give up to save money – and others you will not. Only you can decide.*

6

Jump off the consumer carousel

New isn't always the best. And second-hand is not a pauper's option, it's a thrifty one. Be careful with your money and buy yourself more free time.

Once you catch the second-hand bug you will be amazed at the treasures you can find. Think of what happens when you buy a new car — drive it out of the showroom and you lose thousands!

If the term 'second-hand' conjures up unhappy memories of ill-fitting hand-me-downs and grotty old toys bought from school fairs, think again. Shopping for goods that are second-hand – or 'gently used' or 'pre-loved', if you prefer the eBay euphemisms – can literally save you hundreds if not thousands of pounds. Second-hand items can cost a tenth of their original price or less. Usually, if you can buy it new you can buy it second-hand. What you pay obviously depends in part on luck and the time you are willing to spend looking, but you can shorten the odds by deciding where to look. I'm not a fan of jumble sales because it's unlikely that I will

Here's an idea for you... **If you can't find exactly what you're looking for, customise. Second-hand textiles can be simply altered to fit the bill by anyone with dye or fabric paint. Second-hand furniture can be stripped or painted.**

find the things I want there – I'm not in the market for second-hand toys, bric-a-brac, etc. I occasionally go to garage and boot fairs because they are a good source of sturdy, hand worn tools and even cheap plants. Look in the classified ads, too. Online auctions are useful if you don't get carried away with bidding, but remember to factor in the postage, which can be expensive if you are buying heavy goods.

Charity shops are an excellent source of goods at ridiculously low prices. I have bought wine-making demijohns, solid wooden furniture, velvet curtains, baskets and table linen. Oh, and books; hundreds of books. I admit it: my name is Lynn Huggins-Cooper, and I am a bookaholic. As well as an excellent set of *The Standard Cyclopedia of Modern Agriculture*, I have found other gems on animal husbandry, fencing and productive gardening. Incidentally, books published during World War II, around the 'Dig For Victory' theme, can be invaluable for downshifters because their focus is on producing food and keeping animals cheaply. They often give great suggestions for reusing and recycling household items in the garden. Ignore the suggestions for pesticides and garden chemicals, though – some of the chemicals have now been banned and others are so lethal, they probably should be!

Buying at real auctions – at auction rooms, full of bizarre items, and even stranger 'bidders' – is great fun. I go to two types of auction when I need things. The first type is an auction room that specialises in furniture. Lots of it is rubbish but there are gems to be found. I like solid old furniture – none of the flat-pack crap –

because it looks right in my farmhouse. Modern furniture would look small, mean and out of place. I have bought wonderful carved dressers, presses and cupboards for my house. I like preparing vegetables on an oak table that has seen generations of wear. My yew cupboard, with a marble top, is ideal for preparing pastry – but it cost less than a marble pastry board.

Looking for everyday ways to save money? Check out IDEA 4, *Cheap as chips.*

Try another idea...

The second type of auction is held at the farmers' markets. I stocked myself with hens, bantams, rabbits and quail from such auctions. I have also bought ridiculously cheap bundles of wood, fence posts, wire, hen feeders and rabbit runs. Plus, the contacts you can make while standing round the auction ring are invaluable. Although some of the advice might conflict, it is freely given.

The bottom line is this: if you spend less, you need to work less, because you need less money. It's one of the basic principles of downshifting.

'*Second-hand or vintage? It's all a matter of semantics and snobbery.*'
JUDY CARRUTHERS, vintage clothing market stallholder

Defining idea...

How did
it go?

Q **I'm quite happy to buy clothes second-hand, but I'm not keen for my friends to know. What can I do to avoid them finding out?**

A *The glib answer is, don't tell them! Seriously, though, what are you ashamed of? You are making a decision to use your money wisely, and that's laudable. You are also using the world's resources sensibly by reusing something someone else does not want. That's nothing to be ashamed of! If your friends are dumb enough to be repulsed by second-hand clothes, tell them it's 'retro chic'. Cheap Date, a US magazine, is devoted to what the Americans call 'thrifting' – essentially, many of the fashionistas have discovered the joys of second-hand clothing. Sophie Dahl, the Hilton sisters and Erin O'Connor have all contributed to the magazine. They call it 'vintage', however. Even Vogue recently carried a fashion story about 'thrifting' featuring Kate Moss.*

Q **I'd like to buy goods at auction, but am worried that if I scratch my nose I'll go home with an expensive accordion! How difficult is it to learn the ropes?**

A *Sometimes it's actually hard to make sure the auctioneer has seen you and taken your bid because the action moves so fast! When you register at the auction office, you are given a number, usually on a card. I hold this number in the air to make a bid. Easy! As you are bidding, bear in mind that a bid is binding and final. If you get caught in a bidding war, do not be tempted to go too high in the thrill of the chase. I usually note down the ceiling bids I am prepared to make on paper before I start, to put a dose of reality firmly in front of me. You should also bear in mind that you will pay a percentage of the cost of your item as a 'buyer's premium'.*

7

Cut the crap: decluttering for dummies

As we go through life, we all collect piles of crap that we drag along behind us like Jacob Marley's chains – but the more we have, the more there is to keep clean and tidy. Declutter and free yourself!

We've all watched the TV shows and laughed as lifestyle gurus embarrass people by laying out piles of their stuff for all the world to see. However, how would your home look in the decluttering spotlight?

Once you decide to downshift, a strange thing happens. Even if you weren't a packrat before, you can start to look at things in a new light – that bottle might make a good cloche; suddenly you have a box full in the garage. Or you can hold on to items 'just in case' they come in handy. The piles grow and the cupboards bulge. Soon you are suffocating in a pile of 'things'.

Here's an idea for you... **Save photos – not objects. When you store baby toys, Cub Scout uniforms and tiny shoes, you are trying to hold on to a warm memory. However, a picture can evoke the memory as much as the item itself. If you have a photograph of the object or outfit being used, try to steel yourself to give away the real thing.**

I am, by nature, Queen of the packrats. However, I married a man who is quite the reverse. While for him this is undoubtedly a cause of angst, for me it is a blessing. He marches sternly around in my wake curbing my excesses. (Believe me, the urge to keep things 'just in case' gets worse when you have outbuildings!)

Successful downshifters are resourceful people, clever with their hands and inventive. They make an art form out of reusing and recycling – but it can get out of hand. Then it's time to declutter. We downshift because we want a simpler life, yet the more stuff we have, the more complicated it gets. Speaking from experience, too many things crammed into a house can be oppressive.

Walk around your house – and sheds! – and take a cold hard look. If you are anything like me, there'll be stuff that you haven't used in years. Get rid of it!

Here's how to get started. Walk round with a black sack. There are probably things in every room you can throw out or send to the recyclers. You know the stuff I mean: single socks, old magazines, broken things you have been meaning to fix for months, out of date dried food packets. I guarantee that this bit is really satisfying.

The harder bit is deciding what to give away. Get two large boxes and go into the first room. (A note: do not try to do the whole house at once. Do a room at a time, and do it thoroughly.) Collect together everything that doesn't belong in the room. Dump them in one of the boxes so you can carry it round the house, putting things away in the right place.

Look hard at the things that do belong in the room – for now. If you haven't used an item for a year, or you don't really like it anymore, put it in the second box. This is the box of goods to sell/take to the charity shop. I realised the other day that gathering dust on a shelf in the

> **There are lucrative ways to declutter. IDEA 8, *Supplementing is great for your health*, gives tips on decluttering at a profit.**

Try another idea...

utility room were a microwave egg poacher and a microwave crisp maker. Guess what – I gave away the microwave a year ago and didn't buy a new one because I wanted to rely less on electrical appliances. Needless to say, those goods have now been given away.

Once you have enough stuff gathered together – and it won't take long! – take it to the charity shop straight away. That way you cannot change your mind.

Watch what you bring home. There's no point in decluttering and then filling the space with more stuff. Make sure that when you buy something, you get rid of the item you are replacing. It's not rocket science, but it is important.

Get organised! Think hard about storage options. When you can't find things you need, you get frustrated, and waste time. But be careful that you aren't organising new storage instead of getting rid of things. Remember, even though you can't see the things in the cupboard, they are still there.

Try to store things where you use them. It sounds obvious, but trailing to the utility room for something you need upstairs in the bathroom is a nuisance. Store clean towels in a trunk in the bathroom; tools in boxes or on racks in the shed, etc.

> **'In order to seek one's own direction, one must simplify the mechanics of ordinary, everyday life.'**
> PLATO

Defining idea...

29

How did it go?

Q   **I have a huge bag of household items that are perfectly usable – I just don't need them. Any ideas on where to dispose of them? They are too good for the tip.**

A   *The tip? Nemesis of downshifters! Rather than clogging up landfill sites, decent goods can be sold and the profit used to bolster your downshifter's contingency fund. Goods can also be given to charity shops and welfare organisations or offered to relatives and friends. Can you swap them? That cuts out the consumerism part of getting something new; unfortunately, it doesn't cut down on the clutter!*

Q   **I work from home now as a result of my downsizing, but my desk is buried by a paper mountain! How can I keep control?**

A   *The golden rule is to deal with things as they arrive, on a daily basis. As you open your mail, immediately bin the junk. I find opening mail actually over a waste paper basket helps. File the mail you need to keep, such as bills, work enquiries, etc. every day. Once you have read a newspaper or a magazine, put it straight in the recycling bin or the 'redistribution' box.*

8
Supplementing is great for your health

No matter what you decide to do to downshift – work 'smarter', garden farm or move to a smallholding – putting a little extra money in your pocket doesn't hurt.

For a happy life, we have two choices. We can either find something we love to do, and get paid to do it, or we can become self-sufficient.

My father taught me a lot about the choices in life as I was growing up. He was a fireman. The work was hard, it was dirty, it was emotionally draining – but he loved it and it was a job that really mattered. He was paid to save lives, feel adrenaline rushes and drive a fire engine. What more could a man ask for? He and my mother also taught me about self-sufficiency. They always had at least one allotment, if not more. They taught me by example; I learned more by osmosis than instruction. What I know about growing food – preparing soil, planting and nurturing seeds, taking cuttings – comes from them.

Here's an idea for you... **If you have a large collection of books, DVDs and CDs, think very carefully about whether you will read, watch or listen to them again. If there are any you could do without, think about listing them on Amazon Marketplace. Although eBay is a good online auction site, books and CDs usually reach a better asking price on Amazon. It's easy to sign up for, but be careful that you give accurate descriptions of the condition of your books and CDs or you could end up with bad feedback and no buyers. Package your items carefully and factor the packaging into your total price.**

If you are not fortunate enough to have discovered a job you love, it may have been part of your decision to downshift. Like my dad, I am lucky to be paid to do something I enjoy – writing – and that gives me an incredible sense of well-being and wholeness. I also love to be outside, and nothing feels better than feeding my family on things I have grown myself. Hence our move to a smallholding.

Finding a way to supplement your income, even in small ways, is a great way to give yourself choices. When you are in full-time employment, putting away a little extra each month can help you to build up a fund to enable you to work less – or even to give you six months' or a year's breathing space if you decide to give up employment to move towards a self-sufficient lifestyle.

You may have already decided to give up a paid job for a life of self-sufficiency. But what do you do for money? Most of us need at least a little money for some things, even if we learn to live frugally and provide for most of most of our own needs. Bills still need to be paid, even for the downshifter.

You have a variety of options. They won't make you rich, but they will help towards the price of seeds, bags of corn, and utility bills until you are established. Firstly, you should consider what assets you have to sell and kill two birds with one stone as you declutter. You can take things to a local sale or sell things on eBay (it's easy to register and you'd be amazed to see some of the odd things that sell!).

Fancy starting your own business? Find out what's involved in IDEA 10, *Getting down to business*.

Try another idea...

Another good source of money is plants. You will be growing many plants for yourself, so start off some extras to sell. It is a good idea to specialise, perhaps in herbs, perennials or shrubs. You can sell them through local farmers' markets and give out cards with your contact details. Again, you can also sell via internet auction sites but you will have to think about secure packaging if you are going to send live plants by mail.

Be very clear about what you are doing – are you supplementing your income, or starting a business? If it's the latter, you have to be very careful that the business does not take over your life. It would be very easy to suddenly find that you are working the long hours that made you want to downshift in the first place. And remember, of course, that whatever income you do manage to create by whatever means is liable for tax and declarable as such.

Many people have come to grief thinking the taxman wouldn't be interested in auction sites – he is, and his wrath is merciless. You have been warned!

'A penny saved is a penny earned.'
BENJAMIN FRANKLIN

Defining idea...

How did
it go?

**Q   I love knitting in the evenings and people tell me I'm very skilled
and creative. I don't fancy running a small business as such, but I
need a small income. Do you think I could make my hobby pay?**

A   *If you are looking for a few pounds to supplement an otherwise self-
sufficient lifestyle, this could work. It won't make you rich, but there has
been an upsurge of interest in handcrafted, individual garments. It may be
that you decide to go down the online auction route. You may, however, be
able to find small up-market clothes shops locally to supply with one-off
garments. Just make sure you have calculated your costs carefully so that
you make sufficient profits to see you through those cold, dark winter
evenings!*

**Q   I was reading a magazine article recently about Women's Institute
markets. Would it be worth taking a stall to sell my herbs?**

A   *The Women's Institute runs many markets around the country (look on the
internet for details). At a minimum investment from you, they provide a
venue for many 'home produced' goods including preserves, cakes and
crafts. The people attracted to these sales may well be a great customer
base for your herbs. If you take along home-printed business cards, you
may be able to encourage people to contact you directly. Also, produce
leaflets listing the herbs you are able to supply and giving contact details.
Hand them out with purchases to encourage repeat business.*

9

Happy homebody

Is commuting getting you down? Do workplace politics leave you cold? Consider working from home and leave all that stress behind you.

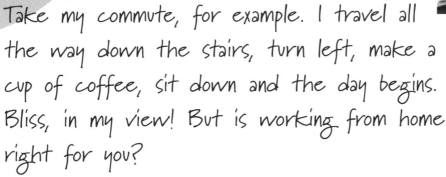

Take my commute, for example. I travel all the way down the stairs, turn left, make a cup of coffee, sit down and the day begins. Bliss, in my view! But is working from home right for you?

Ask yourself, what do you like about the work you are doing now? If you are thinking about downshifting to the country, and moving towards self-sufficiency, constant crowds are probably not your 'thing'. But if you enjoy office banter, revel in 'teambuilding' exercises, delight in office politics, and crave the next instalment of gossip around the water cooler, working from home may not be for you.

However, you may prefer to have more chances to order your own day. Working at home gives you the opportunity to organise your work so that if you need to go to a

Here's an idea for you...

Put out feelers and start developing a support network. Whatever type of work you do, there's sure to be an online community set up to support it, for instance. I belong to several writing communities, and have made good friends who are able to provide sound advice as well as companionship. It is also worth looking for local face-to-face groups in your nearest town. Your local government offices or library may well hold details of these community-based groups.

meeting at school, or visit a nearly empty open garden, you can. That doesn't mean homeworking is all about slacking – you still need to get the work done, but you can do it at a time that suits you and your family.

Being around for my family was a great motivator for me, when I made my decision to work from home full time. My youngest child is six and is happily home schooling.

My teenagers both like having easy access to a parent, too – and not just for handouts! Being available at incidental times of the day gives you the opportunity for many more of the 'casual' chats teenagers have with you in passing – when they tell you about the stuff that really matters in their lives.

ARE YOU LONESOME...?

Working at home can be isolating. Before you decide to work at home, check that you will enjoy the peace and calm. If you feel lonely and crave company, homeworking may not be for you. If you are happy with your own company, go for it. I find that my writing demands quite a high degree of concentration, so I like to minimise distractions – and working at home during the quiet of the day helps me. If I want company, I go out – it's as simple as that.

The main disadvantage of homeworking is the likelihood of distraction. Beware the household tasks that suddenly shout at you as you gaze round the room; shoo away the cats that flop down thunderously on a keyboard, or decide to play football with your equipment; ignore dogs that noisily demand walks – but most of all, let your friends and family know that sometimes you must not be disturbed.

I'm not sure whether some people don't actually believe that you are working because you are at home, but the interruptions are regular. You have to decide which ones are acceptable or welcome – good friends who ring up and ask if they can call in for coffee and won't be offended by a refusal – and which you have to discourage.

I have a writer friend who actually takes her car down the street in the morning so people don't know she is at home. It sounds extreme but it works for her. You must develop your own strategies.

Working from home offers benefits both for you and the environment. See what they are in IDEA 2, *Commuting costs.*

Try another idea...

'*Normal is getting dressed in clothes that you buy for work and driving through traffic in a car that you are still paying for in order to get to the job that you need so you can pay for the clothes, cars and the house that you leave empty all day in order to afford to live in it.*'
ELLEN GOODMAN, columnist

Defining idea...

39

Q **I get loads of e-mails about working from home. They sound a bit too good to be true. Are they worth following up?**

A *Be wary of the proliferation of internet-based 'work from home' schemes: very many of them are scams. Chant the mantra: 'If it sounds too good to be true, it is too good to be true.' Even the ideas that are not scams are not usually worth replying to. They may work to a certain extent, but the returns are poor for many hours worked – and you didn't downshift to spend all day, every day strapped to the computer. You could have stayed at work if that's what you wanted to do – the pay would certainly have been better!*

Q **People see I'm at home all day and think I'm not busy. They're trying to land all manner of jobs on me, like helping with the Brownies and at the community centre. How can I stop them?**

A *Firstly, ask yourself: does it matter what other people think? For me, one of the things I like about my move to the country is taking an active part in the life of the local village. The downside is the amount of times I am asked to bake cakes, run stalls, help with events and organisations, etc. However, I've now learned to be firm with people, reminding them that I do have a job, but I work from home. Just start to say no when you need to.*

10

Getting down to business

Have you always fancied being your own boss and starting your own business? Think carefully about the pros and cons to save you from exchanging one sort of stressful life for another.

You may have decided to combine a downshifted lifestyle with starting your own small business to help you to take control of your life. Make sure you are being realistic.

New start-ups can be exciting, and the thought of being your own boss is attractive. However, think whether you really want to exchange one life-consuming job for another – even if you like The Boss better! It is possible to combine a business start-up with downshifting, but be cautious.

When I got married we were poor students and needed to do things on the cheap. I bought some netting and hand edged it, and made my own veil, stitching freshwater pearls and coral beads all over it. I ended up being commissioned by people via family and friends to make others. I phoned the offices of various wedding magazines and told them about my *unique* work. Photos of my creations appeared in all of the glossies. Voila – I was the proud owner of an organically developed business, growing out of a niche in a specialised market.

Here's an idea for you...

Ignore the scammers and pyramid sellers and search online yourself for ideas about the types of business that might suit you. The Work at Home Moms site (wahm.com) is interesting, and not just for mothers. Entrepreneur.com is another source of low-cost ideas for business start-ups. Remember to keep your BS detector on full alert and be careful if you sign up for any newsletters – they might sell your e-mail address to other companies and leave you with thousands of extra junk mails.

That is the key to combining a business with downshifting. Make sure the business grows out of an interest you have, such as craft working, writing, growing and selling vegetables or whatever it is you enjoy – and are good at. Make sure the business fits into your life, rather than taking it over. If you do decide to start a business as a part of your downshifted lifestyle, think small. If you do not want to think small, you are probably not looking for a simplified life, and you'll probably never be able to truly downshift.

By all means go for a big start-up, supported by venture capital, if that is your dream. However, if you do, forget about spending more quality time with your family or growing your own fruit and vegetables because you simply won't have time.

WHAT CAN I DO?

You can possibly cash in on the e-commerce revolution working from home, depending on what it is you have to sell. For example, eBay is not just used by people supplementing their income and decluttering their houses; there are also people on the site who run full-scale shops. Many of these are people working from home and selling goods they have made themselves, such as candles, woven willow goods, soaps and bath bombs. Others specialise in a particular line of used goods – kitchenalia, toys and models, clothes or books. Others sell specialised goods for a niche market, such as gothic clothing, metaphysical goods, or craft materials.

Can creativity provide you with a home-based business? Look for tips in IDEA 11, *Release your creative self*.

Try another idea...

It costs little to set up an e-shop and you can also sign up to online banking facilities such as Bidpay and Paypal. These charge a fee per transaction, but it means you can accept immediate payment for items rather than waiting for a cheque to clear.

You can also sell goods at markets or even from your home. I know one woman who runs a very successful business from an outbuilding on her smallholding, buying, selling and renting out baby and toddler equipment. I know a farmer's wife who runs a dress exchange in a similar way, keeping a whole area supplied with posh frocks. I also have a friend who sells New Age supplies, such as oils, crystals and books, from a room in her house, mail order only. She targets appropriate publications for advertising and takes stalls at New Age fairs to promote her business.

I know other folks who sell services, such as accounting, tutoring, pet sitting and photography. There are as many 'work at home' jobs as there are downshifters. You just have to find the one that is right for you.

'Opportunity is missed by most because it is dressed in overalls and looks like work.'
THOMAS ALVA EDISON

Defining idea...

Q **How do I stop a home business from taking over my life?**

A *Only you can do it. Learn to say no, and do not always be available (by email or phone). Be strict and separate out the areas of your life to maintain a balance.*

Q **I've successfully exhibited my pictures in galleries and sold some pieces. I would like to develop my work with an idea to illustrating children's books on a freelance basis. Is this pie in the sky or a real possibility?**

A *Obviously you need talent to become an illustrator, but you also need determination and a broad back to bear rejections! Try joining a specialised online community to find out more. The Society of Children's Book Writers and Illustrators (scbwi.org), for instance, is a UK organisation set up to help people who write and illustrate for children, and the advice and resources it offers are invaluable. You won't know until you try!*

11
Release your creative self

No time for that novel you've always wanted to write? Want to take time to look at the scenery – and paint it? Downshifting gives you the chance to get your creative juices flowing.

We all have the capacity for creativity. It may be expressed in many ways — whether that's music, garden design or weaving — but we all need time to connect with our creativity to feel whole.

One of the best things about downshifting for me has been reconnecting with my creative self. That sounds pompous, but it really is as important as that. Unless you are very lucky, your creative skills are unlikely to be used in your everyday working life. You become creatively constipated and your ideas will not flow; you will be unable to think freely and laterally. It takes creative thinking to come at a problem from a fresh direction to find a solution.

You may find time to have a creative hobby, such as scrap booking or painting; but if you downshift, creativity becomes part of your everyday life. The problems you

Here's an idea for you...

Don't get bogged down by some outdated, teacher-engendered view of yourself as 'not artistic'. Allow yourself to explore a variety of different types of creative activity. Book yourself on some taster courses at the local college or community centre, or look at books in the library to find something that inspires you. Remember, it doesn't have to be traditional art: it could be weaving, cooking, web design, graphics, garden design – whatever takes your fancy. Don't forget to look online for inspiration too.

are faced with every day – and let's not gloss this over; they will be many and various – force the creativity cells to spark up and fly. Let's face it, if you have moved to a smallholding in the country and decided to be as self-sufficient as possible, you are not going to want to (or be able to) throw money at problems, or call in immediate specialist help.

As a smallholder, you have to use your innate cunning to solve problems, and that involves creativity. Problem with slugs? The downshifter's answer is more likely to be crushed eggshells and cloches cut from plastic bottles than expensive electrified copper-gizmos. Want to build raised beds? The downshifter is likely to use old boards or planings from the sawmills as bed edgings rather than expensive (and not aesthetically pleasing) plastic edging from the garden centre.

Creativity is the downshifter's best friend. Apart from the problem-solving aspect, creativity can make us more at home inside ourselves. That doesn't mean we all have to rush off on some dippy-hippie body painting retreat – although, actually, that sounds like fun – but it does mean that downshifting gives you the space to think about what you would like to try. There is nobody looking over your shoulder telling you what you can't do, so silence your internal critic and have a go!

Until we moved to our smallholding, I'd never had a go at weaving willow structures, although I'd always fancied it, and admired willow tunnels at open organic gardens. I'd always thought 'I could do that' – but never

Fancy designing and creating living structures from willow? Check out IDEA 43, *Wonderful willow.*

Try another idea...

had. Now I have made both living willow and dry woven structures, including edging for beds, and a living willow igloo. I have planted hundreds of willow whips of different colours, from yellow to purple, and increase my stock each year. If I was not a writer, I think I would probably be happy running courses in creating willow structures and art.

In the renovations we have carried out since we moved here, we have converted the dingy, corridor-like kitchen into a fabulous art and craft studio, where the whole family keeps ongoing projects and craft resources. If the resources are out, on display in baskets and tubs, they inspire you as you pass by, and even just looking at them gives me great pleasure and enriches my life.

We stripped the plaster off the walls (three layers, including the original horse hair, beetle wings and lime!). The mess was horrific, but after many days scrubbing we had sparkly sandstone walls, which I have pointed myself. I filled larger gaps with small fossils. Now, I wouldn't like to do it for a living – it was a labour of love – but without moving to this type of country ramshackle property, it would never have occurred to me to have a go. That's at the heart of downshifting; the way we are constantly prodded by our situation to explore new activities. Have a go – you never know what skills you will discover!

'Creativity is a type of learning process where the teacher and pupil are located in the same individual.'
ARTHUR KOESTLER

Defining idea...

47

How did
it go?

Q **I think I'm pretty creative already, but could I use my skills to earn extra cash? I like making jewellery, for example.**

A *You certainly could: you've got nothing to lose if you try. You could sell your designs online, at markets or to friends. I have an extensive collection of herbs in my garden and could make money by propagating these or creating herbal bath potions (which I also do for fun). I have also sold handmade items at craft fairs in the past. The point is that downshifting gives you the opportunity to explore your creativity and possibly make money in the process.*

Q **I've never been good at arty stuff so it doesn't seem worth trying to do anything creative. What would you suggest for me?**

A *Think again! Creativity isn't just about writing and painting. When you plan your garden, it's a creative act. Daydreaming – an essential part of the downshifted life – is creative because you are letting your imagination flow and play. Even cooking can be creative – it's not just about feeding and fuelling the body; it's also about exploring tastes and textures. In short, don't feel restricted; go for it!*

12

Get fresh in the kitchen

Moving to the country is not going to turn you into a keen cook overnight but when you are faced with all of that fresh produce, bursting with vitamins and minerals, it really is time to become creative in the kitchen.

Many of us fall easily into the trap of buying and cooking pre-prepared meals or 'ready to assemble' meals. As well as being more expensive than fresh food, they have been processed and are therefore likely to have lost some of their goodness.

Most people live busy lives, and food you just unwrap and pop in the oven is an attractive option. It often seems quicker and easier to buy bags of prepared vegetables that just need to be zapped in the microwave. If you live in the city, even if you have a market you can get to in your lunch hour, the fresh produce is not necessarily *that* fresh once it gets to you, and it can be expensive.

Here's an idea for you...

Buy a reconditioned chest freezer and make your own convenience foods. For instance, any glut of tomatoes can be used to make tomato sauce for pasta by simmering the tomatoes with onion and herbs. Freeze it in portion-sized chunks. Shred onions and leeks and freeze them in well-sealed bags. Make fruits (anything left after your jam making!) into purée and freeze in portions for adding to porridge and puddings in the winter. Let your imagination run away with you, and create your own freezer foods for those nights when you are too tired to cook 'properly' after toiling in the garden.

Downshifting to a simpler lifestyle rejects the concept that speed and time saving are always the desirable way to do tasks. In the world where time saving is the ultimate goal, even cooking has become a chore. In the world of the downshifter, eating is the culmination of your efforts, when the seeds you plant and the plants you nurture and harvest are prepared fresh from the ground.

I still buy food from the supermarket, but the more natural food I produce, the more the processed food tastes artificial and like eating cardboard packaging. Until you have eaten strawberries straight from the bed, still warm from the sun, you'll doubtless be satisfied by glossy, imported supermarket strawberries with no flavour. But once you have tasted tiny home grown alpine strawberries, you will be forever converted. The same goes for eggs still hot from the nestbox. The first time we ate eggs from our own 'girls' we went into raptures! It wasn't just because they were produced at home, as if by magic, but also because of the fragrant yellow yolks that were quite unlike the artificially coloured, size-graded creations bought at the supermarket.

Home produced food tastes better. It goes into the pan fresh, and comes out full of flavour. When you produce your own food, you also have a choice about the chemicals you use – or choose not to. Pesticide levels in some commercially produced food can be enormous because of the stringent standards about the appearance of food that major supermarket chains demand from farmers. Personally, I'd rather cut any grotty bits out of my food and know it was free of chemicals. I have made a choice to garden organically – the slugs get a bit, the birds get some, and so do the caterpillars; but so do we.

You cannot overestimate the swell of pride you will feel as you carry your trugs and baskets of produce into the kitchen. Once the food comes inside, you have to think about what to do with it. Actually, food *this* fresh tastes so good you don't have to do anything that complicated. Even if you are a meat eater, it is worth investing in a good vegetarian cookbook because if everything goes well in the garden (and there's no reason why it shouldn't) you will have seasonal gluts, and your kitchen will end up looking like a church in the middle of Harvest Festival. When you are buying seeds, it is worth thinking about what you will make the food into once it grows, and what you will do with your excess produce (preserves, jams, pickling, drying, freezing, etc.), rather than just buying the packets because they look so tempting. Vegetarian cookbooks will give you tips (or look online).

Find out about the foods you can grow for your freezer – and what to make them into – in IDEA 21, *Frozen assets*.

Try another idea...

'**It's difficult to think anything but pleasant thoughts while eating a home-grown tomato.'**
LEWIS GRIZZARD, American comedian

Defining idea...

Q **I rather fancy a big farmhouse kitchen with an Aga. Are Agas easy to run?**

A *People often think that if they downshift, they simply* must *have an Aga-type range cooker. I know many people who have them, but seeing the work needed to use them put me off. Agas are cosy in winter and keep the kitchen snug, but remember that the Aga still throws out heat in the summer, which can be uncomfortable because your kitchen gets stuffy. If you have a solid-fuel Aga, don't forget someone needs to chop, and lug, the wood. Agas take ages to warm up, and cool down, plus the heat levels are not easily adjustable – though I know several people who manage startlingly well. As my skills are more in the garden than the kitchen, I went for a large electric range cooker – many country properties have no gas. I can cook loads of food at once, filling the ovens, which is economical.*

Q **I am keen on growing fruit for making jam. Apart from the obvious, such as strawberries, raspberries and blackberries, what should I plant?**

A *Blackcurrants are easy to grow and give huge yields – great for making juice. Redcurrants are great for jelly – but remember to net them to keep out birds. Any of the hybrid berries, such as tayberries and loganberries, are also a good choice.*

13

Wholefood for the soul

Downshifting is all about improving your quality of life. This includes being good to yourself and stepping off the stress treadmill.

One of the best things about downshifting is the way you become much more centred and 'whole'. You are in control of your life — as much as anyone reliant on Mother Nature can be.

Autonomy gives you an enormous sense of well-being. Many people seek to downshift specifically to achieve personal peace and a sense of calm in a world that's increasingly busy. People trapped in the rat-race try to fill the emptiness at their centre by buying external pleasures, such as designer clothes, jewellery and flashy cars, but at best they only experience a temporary high and the associated debt keeps them on a carousel of needing to earn more to spend more.

Take time to live *in* your body, rather than using it merely as a tool. Sit on the ground and make yourself comfortable. Push your fingers into the soil and feel its texture. Close your eyes and listen to the sounds you hear, then let them slip away. Breathe deeply, feeling the air filling your lungs. Visualise light and warmth filling your body with every intake of breath; picture murky fragments of tension and stress pouring out as you exhale. Feel the warmth of the sun on your face and the crumbly earth between your fingers before coming slowly back to yourself.

Whenever we neglect our inner selves, we are left wanting more. Learning to live a more simple life helps to put you in touch with yourself; it grounds you and makes you fulfilled. Once your 'outer life' – work, social commitments, money – is simplified, you have space to sort out your inner self. Once you are peaceful, you do not feel the need to stay busy and run away from your problems. You deal with them head on, and find out who you really are.

Some people like to find inner peace through meditation. I find my peace outside, hands plunged into the soil. With the earthy smell and the cool dampness, it's as though I have quite literally 'earthed' myself – I feel the nervous energy and stress leak away to be neutralised by the soil. My mind clears and the problems that seemed insurmountable in the house stop boiling around in my head and keep still long enough to be dealt with.

Spending time outside, nurturing plants and animals, and watching things grow helps you to find your place in the scheme of things. Truly experiencing the changing seasons and the turning of the year helps you to feel connected to the rhythms of life. Modern life, in all its hermetically sealed, germ-free existence, makes you feel disjointed and out of synch – even with yourself. This can have an effect on your sleep, your stress levels and ultimately your health.

Get in tune with the seasons and the cadences of the year by reading IDEA 22, _Catch the rhythm: live by the seasons._

Try another idea...

We live in a world of full-on, in-your-face stimulation. We are assaulted by noise and colour wherever we go. We fill the quiet constantly with radios, TVs and other portable devices of entertainment and communication. In the home, household appliances are noisy – vacuum cleaners, blenders, washing machines – and at the office, photocopiers and computers create an insistent background hum.

Noise has been linked to stress, mental disorders and high blood pressure. Develop a habit of quiet. Carve yourself some time to go to a quiet place at some point, *every day*, to give you the chance to calm and centre yourself and your quality of life will soar.

'Gardening is not a rational act. What matters is the immersion of the hands in the earth, that ancient ceremony of which the Pope kissing the tarmac is merely a pallid vestigial remnant. In the spring, at the end of the day, you should smell like dirt.'
MARGARET ATWOOD, Canadian poet and novelist

Defining idea...

How did
it go?

**Q   I have a really busy life! I work from home in a job I love, but we
have three children from teens to tinies and the house is always
noisy! What can I do to create a bit of calm?**

A   *Create a mini 'retreat' time at home and enjoy the silence. Can you
reorganise your working day to provide a proper rest in the middle when
you can go for a walk, or sit and stare, or read for fun (no work related
materials allowed)? Or rope in the teens (for a suitable reward) to take the
little ones out to play while you have a relaxing home spa. It is important
that you build in 'me time', particularly as a parent who works at home and
blurs the boundaries of home and working life.*

**Q   I'm feeling really stressed out at work and am getting to the point
where I just can't cope. I've tried talking to my line manager, but
he just treated it as a bit of a joke, saying that a bit of stress
would help me to meet my deadlines. I dread going into work now,
and my sleep is disturbed. What can I do?**

A   *This behaviour from your manager is unacceptable. You should speak to your
union rep. to find out what help may be available to you at work. Your
manager is shooting himself in the foot because stress is a huge factor in
decreased productivity and time lost through absence. More importantly,
though, you need to take a long hard look at your work/life balance. It sounds
as though work is what defines you at the moment. Consider changing jobs,
thinking about what makes you happy. You may be in your current work
environment because it pays well, or confers high esteem, but is it really what
you want to do with your life? A less pressurised job may suit you, even if it
means a cut in wages. Think hard – you do not want to become burned out,
as happens to so many bright, capable people just like you.*

14

Self-sufficient in suburbia: garden farming

Is it really possible to create a downshifted Utopia without moving to the country? The simple answer is yes. It's all a matter of scale.

Obviously, a large garden is better than a small one if you want to feed yourself, but you can even grow food in an apartment without a garden if you use containers.

Starting off with a 'garden farm' could save you lots of grief – and money – later on if you decide that living off the land is not for you. It's a lot harder to decide that you've made a mistake *after* you've hauled your family miles out into the country, changed the kids' schools and left your old life behind. Garden farming gives you a taster of the delicious food you can produce but with a dose of reality thrown in, in the form of digging in all weathers and arranging for someone to 'hen sit' if you go away for the weekend.

Cottage gardeners in centuries past had riotously attractive gardens that mixed flowers, herbs and ornamentals with fruit and vegetables. As a garden farmer you can do that too. Many fruit and vegetables are attractive in their own right, such as

Here's an idea for you...

When you are planning what to grow, think about what your family likes to eat, and what is expensive. If you have a very small garden, avoid space-greedy plants such as cabbages, sprouts and main crop potatoes, but grow tiny earlies and specialities such as delicious pink fir apples in tubs. Concentrate on expensive delicacies such as asparagus, fruits and sugar snap peas. Be adventurous. Try rare varieties, such as those available from the Henry Doubleday Research Association seed bank.

brightly coloured ruby chard, purple orache and plump terracotta pumpkins. Rhubarb is a great foliage plant, as is curly kale. The best part is you can eat it all!

The key to a productive garden in a small space is cunning. Use all of your surfaces. On fences and walls, grow climbing fruits, such as loganberries and tayberries, espalier apples and peaches. Grow food vertically, such as peas, beans and raspberries, to maximise space. Use willow wigwams to give you extra room. I plant a mixture of sweet peas and beans together – it looks pretty, and attracts pollinating insects too.

Plan your layout carefully, making sure to leave space for a compost heap and a greenhouse or small polytunnel – invaluable for starting off seedlings and overwintering tender plants. The position of your beds needs to be thought through. I prefer to garden in raised beds, which can be made cheaply and easily from planking, and even painted if you like. Don't feel that you have to plant in neat, well-spaced out rows either.

When I lived in London, I intercropped food in my small urban garden, which meant I planted fast growers such as lettuce in between rows of slower growers, so the space wasn't 'wasted'. I have also experimented with block planting rather than rows because it takes up less space, potentially. Grown either way, my crops have been fine and the productivity levels have not been noticeably different either way.

You will have to be careful that your small area does not become 'over-farmed' and worn out. It is even more important for you than for the larger scale smallholder to feed your soil to keep it rich in nutrients. Add lots of well-rotted compost and manure, and make liquid compost by dangling a hessian bag of horse muck into a water butt and leaving it to steep. Water your plants freely with this. I also keep a patch of the herb comfrey (which the bees love) for making liquid feed. Regularly cut back the leafy parts of the plant and put them in an old bucket or tub. I weight mine down with a large heavy slab so the juice squeezes out as the leaves rot down. My dad makes his in an old tea urn so he can turn on a tap and the treacly goodness trickles out, ready to be added to water in a can.

Fancy taking your self-sufficiency ambitions further and growing more? Have a look at IDEA 18, *A lot of scope for growth*.

Try another idea…

You also have to be careful to think about crop rotation. It sounds like something only a large-scale farmer would worry about, but in a small space it is even more important. Basically, you should plan your beds so that you do not grow the same type of crop in the same bed season after season. A particular crop needs a particular type of nutrient, and leaching them from the same soil year after year will impoverish your soil. Not using crop rotation will also make the risk of disease more likely as soil becomes infested with pests or spores from diseased plants. It makes sense to change the bed you use on a yearly rotational basis to avoid these problems.

'A garden is never so good as it will be next year.'
THOMAS COOPER, journalist

Defining idea…

How did it go?

Q **I have a large suburban garden. Can I keep hens, or is that a silly dream?**

A *As long as your garden is securely fenced, you can safely keep a trio of hens. Don't get a cockerel if you have neighbours – they won't thank you for the wake up calls! Invest in a secure hen ark and run to keep your hens safe from urban foxes, dogs and even large cats. Hens are very easy to care for, and the eggs are delicious.*

Q **I have a tiny yard. Is it possible for me to grow anything or should I just wait until I move to a bigger house?**

A *You can grow plants, such as strawberries, blueberries and nectarines, in tubs in your yard and climbers on trellises up the walls. Inside you can grow peppers, indoor tomatoes, even melons and grapes. Consider any conservatories, sunny extensions or even large windowsills – they all make great growing spaces.*

15

Should I stay or should I go? Moving to the country

The countryside has a culture all of its own and life moves at a different pace. This can be wonderful – if you adjust.

Moving from urban areas to the country should be approached as though you are emigrating. Plan to expect a shock to your system.

The countryside has a special energy all of its own, but sometimes you have to look quite hard to see it! Rather than the bright, brash energy of city life, the energy of the countryside throbs along unobtrusively under the surface. 'Incomers' (namely, anyone who has not lived in the area all their lives, and cannot trace their family back to antecedents such as Great Aunt Betsy who was a maid up at the Big House) can find this all a bit baffling and frustrating. They react to the inevitable delays and seeming lack of any sense of urgency with frustration.

If your downshifted home is next to or near farmland, make friends with the farmer sooner rather than later. If you have a relatively small acreage of land, you may find it hard to keep the grass cut, for example, and the local farmer may well be able to help you out for a small fee. It also helps to know when 'things' are going on – the awful stench of silage may only be around for a couple of days a year but you'll definitely want to avoid it coinciding with a garden reception for your daughter's wedding!

Get used to things moving more slowly in a small village. Queues form as people talk about their kids, bunions, the weather – whatever. This can be annoying when you are rushing to send a package to the city people you freelance for, because they are still moving on 'townie time' and don't appreciate the delays. But isn't this different rhythm one of the reasons you moved to the country?

If you are to enjoy rural life, you must do your homework about where you live, who else lives there and what they are like. It is important to scope out the neighbours, especially if you are fairly remote. It is very handy to know there is a friendly face – and, more importantly, willing hands – if you have an emergency. Our neighbours stepped in to take our daughter down to the village to school, for example, when I broke my leg (during a drunken moonlit hedgehog rescue – enough said!).

There are many places to meet locals, including of course the pub, the shops and the local school (if you have children!). There will also be many and varied local events for you to join in with.

When you first arrive, try to be unobtrusive. You only have yourself to blame when people laugh scornfully if you roar into town in your newly purchased 4 x 4 and designer country casuals. Instead, ease in gently. It's hard when folks peer at you and you feel like the new kid in school, but try to think before you speak, too. It's very easy to come across as brash and patronising if you join a group and immediately try to make a mark. Sit back instead; listen and take the measure of the place.

Want to take a course or do some research into moving to the country? Discover what you can do in IDEA 16, _Look before you leap: finding out more._

Try another idea...

You will find many new friends, often in the strangest places. I have some really unusual pals these days, but have learned some very valuable lessons about what will grow locally, raising various types of stock and what works _here_. You don't have to accept everything as though it was handed down on tablets of stone (keep your bullshit detector set to maximum sensitivity – country folks can have a weird sense of humour!) but people who have lived in an area for many years have information and wisdom you will find nowhere else. I even know how to skin, stuff and mount a weasel these days – and they don't teach you _that_ in most cities!

How do you know when you stop being an incomer? Actually, it's unlikely that you ever will, especially to the old die-hards. But you'll know you've been _accepted_ when you find bunches of surplus carrots, baskets of blackberries and dahlias wrapped stylishly in newspaper on your step – they had too many; they were passing: see?

'The best things that can come out of a garden are gifts for other people.'
JAMIE JOBB, author

Defining idea...

Q I wanted to change down to the slower pace of life in the country, but I'm finding the switch very difficult. I go crazy after I call the plumbers for help and they turn up days later! And I even hate the queues at the local shop as people chat. Will I ever adjust?

A *Firstly, give yourself space. It will take you a while to move down a gear. It sounds as though you are giving yourself needless stress. Delays are a fact of life in the country, and you need to get used to it if you stay. Give it time. You may pretty soon find yourself wondering what all the fuss was about – and your blood pressure will feel the benefit!*

Q I've given up a lengthy commute in favour of working from home but my mind still whirls with all the things I need to do. How can I make myself slow down?

A *Make sure you have not given up the commute only to let other 'busy' things fill the time you would have spent driving. Build in extra time to relax. This is the only way your internal rhythms will slow. I schedule regular bouts of 'staring out of the window blankly' time, second favourite only to 'lying about on the grass staring at the sky' time.*

16

Look before you leap: finding out more

If you are wondering how to get started with downshifting, becoming self-sufficient or productive gardening, you need to do your research.

There are many organisations, books, websites and courses out there designed to help you. Here's the pick of the bunch.

BOOKS

I always start with books. Apart from being a writer, I'm a voracious reader. If you are like me, you'll like to pore over them, and dream your dreams – and never more so than with downshifting. Relevant books vary from extensive manuals to pamphlets, but they have all been really useful to me. You will find most of these books at the library, or you may prefer to buy them (many turn up in second-hand bookshops).

You won't get far on a book list about downshifting without bumping into John Seymour's *Complete Guide to Self-Sufficiency* (ISBN: 0-751-36442-8) in one imprint or

Here's an idea for you... **Join a local allotment, community gardening or smallholding association. Apart from the material benefits, such as cheap seeds, tools, etc., there is a wealth of knowledge among members. You could even set up a 'lend and exchange' group, with seed swapping and larger tool loans, on a co-operative basis with fellow members.**

another. This weighty tome covers everything from allotment gardening to scything and thatching. It has such a wealth of information that I would recommend it above most others.

Home Farm by Paul Heiney (ISBN: 0-751-30461-1) is another favourite of mine. It has lots of well-organised information and is easy to dip into at the level you want – be it garden farm, home farm or smallholding. The pictures – many of the author and his family – are great for fuelling dreams of what might be.

Henry Doubleday Research Association, *Encyclopaedia of Organic Gardening* (ISBN: 0-751-33381-6) is a 'must have' for me – and anyone who wants to garden organically. It is packed with useful, hands-on information and I return to it often. If organic gardening is of interest to you, you should join the HDRA or similar organisation. Apart from being a source of invaluable advice, you can also join the Heritage Seed Library and gain access to many heritage varieties of delicious vegetables that you just cannot buy. You can also very cheaply buy pamphlets that tell you everything you need to know to get started as an organic gardener.

Cottage Economy by William Corbett (ISBN: 0-953-83250-3) is a classic. The book was written in the 19th century with a view to improving the health of country labourers, but don't let that put you off. It has lots of useful – and cheap – ideas, and Corbett was a grumpy old bugger, so it makes for quite an amusing read!

Food For Free by Richard Mabey
(ISBN: 0-00219060-5),
together with its companion *Plants
With a Purpose*, enriched the childhood
of my sister and I as we gathered all manner
of wild foods and lugged them home, much to my mother's horror. It's invaluable.

Thinking about expanding your plans? Find out what's involved in IDEA 19, *Scaling up: buying a smallholding.*

Try another idea...

I could go on, as a book addict. But you get the idea. Read the books, dipping in and out to get an idea of what is – or can be – involved in becoming more self-sufficient at the level that suits you and your family.

MAGAZINES

Without doubt, the number one 'must have' magazine for downshifting gardeners is *Kitchen Garden Magazine*. I've subscribed since I read the first issue and still wait eagerly for the magazine to arrive each month. It's full of 'readers' gardens' and allotments. As well as expert advice on growing, it has contributions from Sue Hammon, a chicken expert. Sue runs the Wernlas Collection, a supplier of rare breed chickens. Her columns have been invaluable to me as I have set up new trios of hens and bantams, etc.

A new magazine, *Grow Your Own*, published by
Matthew Tudor, is also proving useful.

Country Smallholding is an interesting buy, with
real life stories, and *Smallholder* magazine has
some useful articles.

*'Learning is not compulsory...
neither is survival.'*
W. EDWARDS DEMING,
Management guru

Defining idea...

I have a set (bought second-hand) of a part-work I remember my parents collecting week by week in the 1970s. It's called *Grow Your Own* and it's well worth looking out for because it is full of practical, inexpensive ideas for growing food in the garden.

WEBSITES AND FORUMS

Useful sites I know include rivercottage.net, countrysmallholding.com, smallholder.co.uk, and thekitchengarden.co.uk. They are all packed with great ideas. You could, of course, do worse than join my own forum ('Downshifting to the good life' on yahoo groups) and chat with others following the downshifting dream.

COURSES

Many courses are available at agricultural colleges. Search for colleges near to you on the internet. You can also search for specific local courses in green woodworking, willow weaving, organic gardening and the like.

Q   **How can I find out about allotments and community garden associations?**

How did it go?

A   *You can ask local people who have allotments or you can usually find information and leaflets at local gardening shows and displays. Online, you can find out more about allotments from The National Society of Allotment and Leisure Gardeners (nsalg.org) or at Allotments UK (allotments-uk.com); in the USA at Capital District Community Gardens (cdcg.org/index.html); and all over Europe at City Farmer (cityfarmer.org/subeurope.html).*

Q   **I've picked up a couple of really old gardening books published during World War II on a kind of 'Dig For Victory' theme. Can I follow any of the advice or are they just quaint insights into the past?**

A   *I love these books and fall upon them with glee at garage sales, church fairs and second-hand bookshops. The great thing about them is they tried to do everything 'on the cheap' and that warms my downshifted soul! The main focus is, of course, on growing food cheaply but I have also used their instructions to make paths and beds. The only bit that makes me cringe is advice on the use of some chemicals. Many of these are no longer available, having been withdrawn from the market as potentially unsafe.*

17

Cabin fever families: downshifting with children

Many people who decide to downshift have kids. In fact, your kids may well be the reason you decide to downshift. What's the downshifting experience like for them – rural heaven or pastoral purgatory?

With its generally lower levels of pollution, lower crime levels, and space and freedom to be outdoors, the countryside is an attractive option to some parents who see their children becoming prisoners in their own urban homes.

The strong sense of community in rural areas supports family life. When everyone knows everyone else (and not only their names but also their lineage and, I suspect, blood group and sexual preferences!) you feel safer about letting your children out of your sight. It's not because bad things don't happen in the countryside; they do –

Here's an idea for you... **Involve your children in the decision to downshift – and how far you take it. Draw up a list of pros and cons together, and discuss them fully. Air any qualms openly. Talk to other families who have downshifted to get views from other children of a comparable age to your own. (You can contact other families via downshifting forums, smallholding groups, etc.)**

paedophiles can be found anywhere and children will get into dangerous situations whether they are playing on urban building sites or around farm machinery. The difference is that in a small village people know the children and are more likely to keep an eye on them and let you know what's going on.

If you have very young children (under five), downshifting is great. Your children will still have access to toddler groups and playgroups, as in the city. However, the trendy baby-gymnastics, violin-playing, 'make a baby genius' groups, beloved of the professional classes in the city, are in very short supply – which I see as a good thing!

Downshifting gives you the time to enjoy your children. When you are out at work full time, you may see your child for just a few rushed moments in the morning on the way to the child minder, and then for half an hour before bed at night. Do you really want such a limited input in your child's life? Downshifting gives you the opportunity to organize your time so you can go pond dipping on a bright spring day, and work alongside tiny pairs of hands in the garden. That's priceless! Even if you enjoy your work, it can't be compared with the pleasure you get from spending unrestricted time with your children.

For children starting school, having downshifted parents is still a boon. You are there to drop them off; you are there at home time. Whether your children are six or sixteen, they still need adult ears to listen carefully to the story of their day. The cup of coffee I have at 4 p.m. with my sixteen-year-old daughter keeps me in touch with the vagaries of teenage girl angst. You are still busy as a downshifted parent, but you are always available. Whether you are in a field spreading compost, or working from a study at home, your children know they can get hold of you when the inevitable crises loom.

Are your family going along with your ideas? It's important that they do so check it out with IDEA 3, *All aboard?*

Try another idea...

School-aged children in the country probably get more freedom than their urban counterparts. Where traffic is less of a worry, it is easier for older schoolchildren to cycle to their friends' houses and there's more space for ballgames and den building. There is also likely to be a variety of clubs for children of this age group, run by the school, church and community centre.

Teenage children can find downshifting more of a challenge. If you are moving somewhere very remote, be aware of the strain this will put on your teenager. You will have thought about their journey to school, no doubt, but don't forget the difficulties he or she may face socially – and be prepared to do lots of chauffeuring.

'Learn wisdom from the ways of a seedling. A seedling which is never hardened off through stressful situations will never become a strong productive plant.'
STEPHEN SIGMUND, journalist and strategic communications specialist

Defining idea...

73

How did it go?

Q **I have an idyllic vision of me and my three-year-old running through meadows, birdwatching, pond dipping, etc. Is that being overly romantic?**

A *Not at all! You can't guarantee the sun will shine, but even dancing in squelchy mud and puddle splashing have their pleasures. You will still have many demands on your time, especially if you work from home and have a productive garden, but you will be able to be spontaneous because you will be on hand.*

Q **I work long hours, I'm stressed and tired, and I feel I'm missing out on family life. Downshifting is my dream but how can I overcome the worry that I'll deprive my kids of the things other kids their age want – designer label trainers, the latest toys? If we downshift I just won't be able to afford them.**

A *Step back and ask yourself: can you afford these things now if they're coming at a cost of your health and no time with your family? Children are very adaptable. At eighteen and sixteen my eldest kids don't ask for 'designer wear'. They enjoy buying 'vintage' clothing, which makes them far more individualistic! You will be surprised by how soon the desire for these things leaves your kids – if it was ever there in the first place. Sometimes, we project our own consumer-driven desires onto our children. If they see that you aren't obsessed by the latest gadget they will soon get the message – children learn more by what we do than what we say, as the old adage goes.*

18

A lot of scope for growth

Allotments are of vital importance, giving many urban dwellers and those with tiny gardens an opportunity to become at least partially self-sufficient.

Following World War II, many thousands of acres of land — including parks — were put down to allotments. Sadly today many are disappearing under housing and road schemes.

I'm biased. I grew up on an allotment. No, my parents didn't dump me there to go feral! Rather, they were the proud owners of two and a half allotments that were brimming with produce and won prizes.

The pleasure of working in the fresh air and the satisfaction of harvesting food you have planted and cared for is almost primal. If you don't have a large garden, an allotment is the ideal solution.

Basically, an allotment is a rented strip of land for the cultivation of crops. Patchworks can be seen along railway embankments all round the country. They appear in unlikely places, tucked in among houses and poked in behind school playing fields. Allotments are administered by local councils, and if you want one you have to put your name on a waiting list for a plot. There are generally rules

Here's an idea for you...

Many plots on offer will be choked with weeds. Divide the allotment into 'bite-sized chunks' and beg old carpets from friends and family. They will think you are mad, but the carpets can be laid on weedy areas to block the light and kill off weeds. This makes it easier to dig over and remove roots when the time comes to cultivate the area.

about what you can and cannot do on your plot. You will be given a list when you take over your allotment.

Allotments are no longer purely the province of the grey gardening brigade, although they are certainly still well represented. Huge ranges of people are now taking on allotment gardens to provide healthy food for their families. Many allotment holders have children who are given their own plot to grow child-friendly favourites such as pumpkins for Hallowe'en and huge nodding sunflowers. These are the gardeners of tomorrow.

It's so exciting when you get your letter telling you that you have reached the top of the waiting list and a plot is available. Don't get carried away, though. There are a few points you need to consider before you sign for the plot.

Think about site security. Vandalism and theft are heartbreaking realities on the allotments. It is truly awful to arrive at the plot to find your greenhouse smashed and your plants uprooted. Therefore, if possible, take a site that is fenced. If it is also surrounded by houses, that is a great help. Something else that deters the yobs is if the site is active, with people working their plots for much of the time.

Think about access to the site. Will you be able to walk there, or will you rely on a car? If so, what parking is available? If you have to walk miles with tools and compost – and even heavy crops – you will soon get fed up.

Is there a supply of water near your plot? You can (and should) add water butts to your plot, but a source of water nearby will help to get you started. It's also the allotment equivalent of the office water cooler, where you get to meet old hands and learn about what does and does not grow well on the site.

Want to know how to create a productive garden? Learn how in IDEA 24, *The best laid plans...*

Try another idea...

If you have a choice of plots, don't take on a larger size than you can handle. It is easy in a fit of enthusiasm to take on a huge plot and find you cannot cultivate it all. A word of warning – don't try to cultivate the whole plot at once; get an area up and running – planted and productive – before you move on to the next area. Otherwise, you may get discouraged and give up as you are not seeing any benefits. A few strawberries or fresh carrots will keep your spirits up and get you motivated.

It is worth adding a small secure shed to your plot to hold your tools because it gets annoying to have to carry your tools backwards and forwards. Adding a small primus stove and a kettle to your shed means you have somewhere to ruminate and survey the land, too! Sheds can be bought cheaply second-hand.

A second-hand greenhouse would also make an invaluable addition to the allotment. This extends the growing season and gives you a place to start off seedlings. Again, these can be bought cheaply. If possible, buy a second-hand greenhouse that you have to take apart because you will be able to make notes about how to put it back together again.

'Happiness is not in the mere possession of money; it lies in the joy of achievement, in the thrill of creative effort.'
FRANKLIN D. ROOSEVELT

Defining idea...

How did it go?

Q **I'd like to grow a few flowers on the allotment, to cut for vases. Do people do this, or are allotments just for fruit and vegetables?**

A *You can grow anything at an allotment – it's not just marrows and prize leeks! Flowers for cutting is a great idea. Look at Sarah Raven's book* The Cutting Garden *for ideas on how to get established. You can also grow plants to transplant into your garden, such as alpines and bedding.*

Q **I want to build a path down the middle of the allotment. Is gravel a good idea?**

A *Gravel is fine for walking on, but unless you put sides on the path the gravel will spread on your beds. It is also really hard to push a wheelbarrow through gravel. Think about laying paving slabs bedded into the soil. Look in the classified ads and you will find them second-hand.*

19

Scaling up: buying a smallholding

You have been growing vegetables and fruit for some time; you may even have some chickens. If you do decide to go the whole hog and buy a smallholding, what should you look for?

In the 1970s, there was a boom of urbanites moving to the country. In those days, derelict cottages with vast tracts of land could be bought for a song, and the new age of 'back to the land' pioneers began.

Some early downshifters thrived, but for others it was a Utopian dream and they were ill-prepared for the reality. Lack of experience and the enormity of what they had taken on overwhelmed them. Many gave up and trudged back to town.

How can *you* avoid this? Firstly, be prepared and go into it with your eyes wide open. Scour the downshifting websites and visit smallholdings and open farms to get a feel for the life. Then you need to find the right smallholding for *you*. Check out different regions; drive around and take trips to find the areas you prefer.

Here's an idea for you... **Take a holiday in winter on a working farm in an area you favour. The trip won't give you a definitive experience, but it will give you an important taste of winter in the country. The days will be short and probably bitterly cold. Spend the majority of your time outside to see how it feels. Remember that livestock needs feeding and tending even in deep snow and high winds, and chores still need to be done. Look on this as an initiation!**

Think about the type of smallholding you want to run. If you want to keep animals, uneven or steep fields are fine, especially for goats and sheep. If you mainly want to cultivate crops – especially in sufficient quantities to sell – you will need flatter land that's easier to work.

When you find a property, go several times and preferably in different weather. A smallholding on a summer's day may appear delightful, but it could be a much bleaker place in gales and driving rain! Walk round the land as well as looking at the house and any buildings. Look at water supplies and fencing. Even if the fencing is falling down, it needn't put you off – but it does need to be factored in to the value you put on the smallholding, and what you are willing to pay. Get an idea of what it will cost to put anything right.

If you like the place and put in an offer, pay for a detailed survey. You may find many faults. Many old rural properties have been bodged together during the course of many years – even centuries – which is part of their charm. However, rubble walls will have been built before damp-proof courses arrived and attractive old beams may be full of rot. The survey results needn't put you off; they will just give you an idea of what you are getting into and what remedial costs may be required.

Check the utilities connected to the house. Water is, of course, imperative – but does the property have mains water, or is it served by a well, bore hole or spring? In remote areas, mains water may not be available. Wells can dry up in hot weather. Be prepared to have any water tested for purity if necessary. If your water is not mains supplied, you will need to have it checked regularly anyway to avoid stomach upsets.

Need to know how to clear the ground for your garden? Find strategies in IDEA 25, *Little weed!*

Try another idea...

Whilst thinking about water, check for flooding hazards. What is the level of the land surrounding the house? Check that run-off rainwater will not flood the house from roadways or banks, for example, and don't overlook any watermarks on outside walls.

You should also consider what sort of heating and lighting is available. Many properties in rural areas are without gas because of the cost of piping in a supply. We have no gas supply, but we have oil fired central heating and wonderful open fires. If you consider relying on solid fuel for all your heating and cooking needs, be realistic because quite a lot of maintenance is involved. How much time do you want to spend chopping wood? Small amounts are fine (as the saying goes, it keeps you warm twice – once in the chopping and once in the burning), but large amounts take an inordinate amount of time. It's exhausting, too – and that's without hauling the unchopped wood.

It is also worth thinking about solar or wind power. Generous grants may be available for installation costs. We are currently adding both types of power not just because they are green energy sources, but also to give us an alternative source of energy to compensate for our tenuous connection to the national grid.

'The trouble with the rat race is that even if you win, you're still a rat.'
LILY TOMLIN, comedian and actress

Defining idea...

How did it go?

Q **I have seen a property I like, but it needs lots of work. Should I hold out for a property in better condition?**

A *You tend to get what you pay for. Had we bought a converted, ready-to-live-in house, we couldn't have paid the mortgage. Smallholders have to be well steeped in the values of deferred gratification! Being a 'fixer-upper' gives a great feeling of personal satisfaction, but only you know the amount of work you are prepared to do.*

Q **The place I've seen that I like is high on a windy hillside. Should I be concerned?**

A *Altitude is an important factor in growing crops. We live at 750 ft above sea level and that even lengthens the reach of winter snows! The growing season tends to be shorter above 500 ft. On the other hand, higher land has the advantage of being cheaper, particularly if more exposed. It's a fine balance.*

20

The home run

Once you become self-sufficient with food and other produce, you start to look closely at taking control of other areas of your life, including the education of your children.

If you have children, you may wonder if perhaps you would be better being self-sufficient in the education your children receive. Home schooling may be the answer.

Some parents home school because they are unsatisfied with the school system, but for most home schooling families this is not the case. People decide to home school because they want to integrate their child's education into the rest of their lives – not in a box marked 'education', where lessons of a predetermined length are conducted whether or not a child is interested in the way they are delivered.

School-based education is not compulsory but it is every child's right to receive an education suitable for his or her age and ability. Check out what your rights are before you take the plunge. Education Otherwise (education-otherwise.org/index.htm), an organisation that supports home schooling families, will give you the information and advice you need.

Here's an idea for you...

Devise a system for keeping a record of what your child learns. As well as being a good way to convince the authorities that you are providing a balanced education, it gives you a great account to look back on. This doesn't mean sheaves of paperwork. I just make notes in a big desk diary of the things we do every day. Make sure you date any written work to show your child's progress.

By their very nature, schools are about conformity. As there are a large number of children in a class, for the class to function properly and the teacher to deliver the curriculum, children must spend a great deal of time passively waiting for others to catch up or rushing to finish their work because others are waiting for them.

Children at school no longer learn by doing 'projects' in a way you might remember fondly from your own early school days. These have been lost in the rush to prepare for the ever-present assessment tests that loom over the teachers, children and school administrators alike. Much of what is good and enriching has been lost as a result, and children are under extreme pressure to succeed. Only in schools where teachers, already hard pressed, give up hours of their own personal time (and there are many of these wonderful people) do children enjoy the drama clubs, art and craft groups and nature study time we all took for granted. I know because I used to be a teacher and, in a test-driven curriculum, the efforts we put in to nurture 'the whole child' were punishing.

Home schoolers make everything into a learning activity. If you think about it, this is how you probably act already with your children. If you are in the garden, you are talking about how plants grow from seeds; how they need the light to grow and make their energy; and that without water, plants will die. You talk about the insects pollinating the flowers so that fruit is made – and your child sees it happen. That discussion alone makes up a large chunk of the primary school science curriculum.

If you are in the kitchen cooking (food technology – science, hygiene, food groups, nutrition) you weigh things out (maths – ratios, capacities) together and talk about what you are doing and what is happening. That's integrated learning.

Worried about how the children will adjust to life in the country? Read IDEA 17, Cabin fever families: downshifting with children.

Try another idea...

If you home school, you can gear education to the learning styles of your children. You will be able to address your child's strengths and weaknesses and teach accordingly, because home schooling gives you flexibility. There are curriculums widely available for home schoolers – so don't think you have to reinvent the wheel, unless you want to!

If you are thinking about home schooling, you must be brutally honest with yourself. Are you prepared to take on the massive commitment to your child's education? Do you find teaching comes naturally, or do you get easily irritated when your child does not understand something? Of course, as a downshifted parent you are more able to organize time to teach your child – something you could not have done if you were out at work full time.

You may worry that your child will miss out on companionship if you home school, but this needn't be the case. You can invite other children round for tea and to play. You can, of course, also join a network with other parents who home school and do 'field trips' together to zoos, art galleries and parks if you choose. And there are always local clubs for children.

'Being a parent is hard enough. Being a home educating parent is even harder. But the hardest thing of all must surely be being a home educating parent who has little contact with others.'
ROSS MOUNTNEY, home educator

Defining idea...

How did it go?

Q **Do I have to teach my child from 9–3.30, like a school does?**

A *Certainly not! When you teach is up to you. Few home schooled children are taught for a 'school day'. With only one pupil it is easy to teach what your child needs to know in fewer hours. This leaves lots of time free for creative and enriching activities, and relaxation, which is something children have forgotten how to do.*

Q **Will people think I am weird – or worse, that my child is – if I home school?**

A *Do you really care? As a downshifter, people may well think your life is different to theirs anyway. Some family members and friends may just feel they have to share their negative feelings with you, but just be polite and let them know firmly that home schooling is your choice for your child. If you can be bothered, show them your child's work at intervals to reassure them that your child is learning well.*

21

Frozen assets

So you've grown a bumper crop of fruit and vegetables. You've made jam, pickles, chutney and wine. What else can you do to stop your crops going to waste? You can freeze them.

Vegetables and fruit tend to freeze well, but it is important to freeze them fresh from the ground to retain the taste and nutrients.

Vegetables are best harvested when young and tender for freezing. Pick them in the morning, and prepare them immediately while they are fresh. It is better to prepare small amounts and have flavoursome, fresh vegetables than to wait for a larger batch and end up with tired vegetables that are barely worth storing. They should be frozen quickly.

PREPARING VEGETABLES FOR FREEZING

Blanching vegetables – If you want vegetables to last a long time once they are frozen, they should be blanched before freezing. That means cooked briefly at a high heat to stop the enzymes that affect taste and appearance from working. They can be stored unblanched for up to three months, but after this time they may start to deteriorate.

Here's an idea for you...

If you have room, buy a cheap second-hand chest freezer just for your produce. Keep it separate from your kitchen freezer. If you have a smallholding that has outbuildings with an electrical supply, keep it there. You can often buy these from freezer produce stores that are upgrading their stock.

Vegetables may be blanched by steam or water. Don't blanch spinach or other leafy vegetables with steam as it makes them mat together unpleasantly. With other vegetables, steaming conserves minerals and vitamins but it takes longer than blanching in water. Blanching needs to be carefully timed, or you can end up with soggy vegetables. After blanching, vegetables must be chilled quickly, so put them in cold water. They need to be chilled right through, or they continue to cook and can become mushy. Vegetables take roughly the same time to chill as they did to blanch. They need to be drained and dried before packing, or ice crystals form, and the vegetables will suffer from freezer burn. Lay them on kitchen paper for a while before packaging them.

To steam blanch vegetables, use a standard vegetable steamer that is used for cooking. Time the blanching from the moment when steam escapes from under the saucepan lid.

Purée and sauces – Another option is to prepare vegetables as a purée or sauce. Tomatoes puréed in this way are great for fresh 'fast food' as they can be prepared and frozen in batches to be added to pasta sauces, curry, chilli con carne, etc. Onions can be chopped finely in a blender, then added, straight from the freezer, to soups, stews and other dishes. The key is to freeze these 'fast foods' in small, one-meal amounts. Purée can also be frozen in ice cube containers for heating and serving to babies or adding in small quantities to soups and stews for extra flavour and goodness. After they have frozen solid, push them out of the ice cube container and pack them into freezer bags.

Want to start making preserves as well as freezing food? Check out IDEA 33, *Hitting the bottle.*

Try another idea...

Complete meals – You can, of course, also make a double batch of meals each time you cook using your own produce. The second portion can be frozen as a quick meal for when you come in exhausted from the garden and don't feel like cooking.

PREPARING FRUIT FOR FREEZING

Always choose top-quality, firm fruit for freezing. Over-ripe fruit turns to mush as it defrosts. Berry fruits (such as raspberries and blackberries, along with all the hybrid berries like tayberries and loganberries) are some of the best fruit to freeze as they retain so much flavour.

Freeze fruit on the same day as it is picked, as soon as possible, to retain flavour and firmness. Wash the fruit in chilled water before freezing. This firms it up and will stop the fruit from becoming squishy.

'Always take a good look at what you're about to eat. It's not so important to know what it is, but it's critical to know what it was.'
ANON

Defining idea...

You can freeze fruit using several methods:

Unsweetened dry method – Basically, all you do is wash and drain the fruit and pack it into bags or plastic containers. I prefer to lay my fruit (such as berries) on a tray and 'open freeze' it before packing it into bags once it is frozen. This stops the fruit from sticking together in clumps, which makes it misshapen and squishy as it defrosts.

Puréed and sweetened – Tart berries, such as blackberries, gooseberries and red- or blackcurrants, can be crushed with sugar before freezing to make a sweetened purée. This can be used for desserts, or as a sauce for ice cream, or added to summer puddings and crumbles or pies.

Again, freeze fruit in small quantities for convenient use in recipes.

How did it go?

Q   I've got pounds of strawberries but I don't want to freeze them as they are because they go a bit sloppy. What else can I do with them?

A   How about making strawberry ice? Crush about a kilo of strawberries roughly with the back of a spoon and add the juice of an orange. Boil 140 ml of water with 250 g of sugar in a pan. Cool this syrup and stir it into the strawberry and juice mixture. Freeze the mixture until it is firm and serve with mint leaves.

Q   Can I freeze herbs? I have lots but don't really want to dry them all.

A   Herbs can be chopped and frozen in bags, or chopped and pushed into ice cube moulds for adding to stews and soups. Herbs such as mint and lemon verbena or lemon balm can also be added in sprigs to water filled ice cube moulds. Added to iced tea or lemonade these are delicious.

22

Catch the rhythm:
live by the seasons

**Animals and plants work with the rhythms of the year.
We, as humans, are programmed to do the same.**

As a downshifter, you will learn to
appreciate the four seasons and the delights —
and challenges — that come with each one.

If you live in the town and work in an office the seasons can pass by almost without you noticing. The only difference is that, if you're lucky, you get to potter in the garden for half an hour after dinner in summer.

It is a very different life for downshifters. You fall into the routine provided by nature, not imposed by working conditions or workplace rules. You will learn to enjoy the changes that each season brings, and find yourself in tune with the turning wheel of the year.

Try to avoid the trap some downshifters fall into: they try to maintain a working week similar to the week they had before they downshifted. They see their new life as replacing their old job. I think this may be so that they do not feel guilty; it's a *work ethic* kick.

Keep a journal of the jobs you do in your garden, how they go and how the garden changes with the seasons. Add sketches if you feel like it. It may not be (nor may you *want* it to be) *The Country Diary Of An Edwardian Lady*, but flicking back over the pages will help you get a sense of the changing seasons and your place within their rhythms.

When things are not growing much, because it's cold and weather conditions are poor, you can spend time making things indoors, such as crafts to sell or perhaps a new chicken coop, put together in the shed or outbuilding. You can take time to reflect upon your successes and challenges, and think about how you can change things for the better. You can even – shock, horror – spend the time just reading or dreaming by the fire – it's allowed!

Our bodies respond to the seasons. As we add more layers of clothes to our bodies with the coming of the colder weather, we can feel a sluggishness setting in as the days shorten. Some people suffer from seasonal affective disorder, an extreme version of this feeling. Getting outside and working in the garden, perhaps digging new beds, can help to improve this condition. It increases the amount of daylight that you are exposed to and this helps to alleviate symptoms.

Conversely, as the days lengthen, and the sap is rising in nature so fast you can hear it crackle, you experience a jolt of energy. Spring is approaching like a soft green juggernaut, and the gardener must spring into action.

You plant seeds when the soil warms – I tend to test it with my hands pressed against the soil, waiting for that 'bone cold' that seeps into your body from chilled earth to pass. I know other folks who walk on soil barefoot to see if the earth is ready – again, waiting for the ground to be warm enough so the cold doesn't chill the bones in your feet. I even knew one old man who tested his beds with his bare buttocks – he grew lovely crops, but strangely enough, no one wanted to eat them.

DON'T FORCE IT!

Just because you are used to buying strawberries from the supermarket in January doesn't mean you need to try to grow them then, using all manner of cunning devices and light boxes. The Victorian kitchen gardeners, who supplied the 'Big House' with pineapples for the table, spent countless man hours on producing few fruits, at a huge financial cost after laying in complex heating systems in their conservatories. They did it basically to show off how rich the lord of the manor was. In Victorian times, pineapples had a great 'wow' factor. Today, although growing pineapples under cover is possible, the rather more humble kitchen garden created by the downshifter should arguably be more concerned with establishing a good supply of seasonal fruit and vegetables, and enjoying each season as it comes.

Think about it: salad crops begin to lose their allure as the days shorten and our bodies crave warming, stodgier fare. Traditional salad crops grow less well in winter, even under cover unless you add quite a bit of heat. But the root crops that grow so well, and are ready for harvest in the winter gain in value as we think about making warming stews and soups.

The gluts of produce you harvest as the season progresses can be frozen (either as they are or rendered into sauces), bottled, pickled or preserved. There's nothing more likely to evoke the pleasures of warmer days on a dark winter's night than a pot of home-made strawberry jam with the lid popped off to release the sweet fragrance of summer.

If you want to be more in tune with natural rhythms and cycles, read IDEA 13, *Wholefood for the soul.*

Try another idea...

'*Be a good animal. True to your instincts.*'
D. H. LAWRENCE

Defining idea...

How did
it go?

Q **I've tried this 'feeling the soil to see if it's warm' thing and it just feels cold and wet to me! Isn't there something more scientific I can use?**

A *You can buy a soil thermometer very cheaply at most garden centres – and also from online gardening stores. These thermometers are useful if you find it difficult to judge the readiness of the soil with your hands – or other extremities!*

Q **I take time to enjoy the passing seasons and have begun recording the rhythms of my plants with a camera. Besides locking them away in an album, any ideas of what I can do with the photos?**

A *You could enlarge and frame them, make a calendar, coasters ... the list is endless! In addition, if you find you have a flair for this type of photography, you may be able to sell your shots to magazines and newspapers. Approach local publications first, targeting their gardening and wildlife features.*

23

Tool time

You can make your life much easier if you have the right tools for the job. As a downshifter, you need to know you've got what it takes in your shed.

You are likely to already have most of the basic tools you need to work your vegetable garden, but let's run through a checklist of must-haves.

Spade – For digging over land, you need a spade. Make sure you choose one that feels comfortable in your hands and isn't too heavy for you, or you will tire faster. For the same ergonomic reasons, make sure your spade is the right length – if you are tall, a standard length spade may cause you to stoop and that will make your back ache. A stainless steel blade is good in clay soil because the sticky earth slides off more easily. I have traditional spades and a 'navvy' spade with a pointed tip, which breaks new ground, especially grassland, more easily.

Fork – Forks are great for digging sticky soil, such as clay, or soil that is full of stones. They are also useful for spreading manure and compost, and for breaking down big clods of earth into a finer tilth. Your fork is ideal for turning the compost heap, to aerate it; for digging up potatoes, and for digging out perennial weed roots.

Make a rack for your tools from planks and brackets fixed to the shed wall and keep them hung in place. If you can find them easily, rather than having to rummage about in the shed, you are more likely to use the correct tool for the job. Thus you won't damage tools, or yourself, as you try to cut wire with secateurs because you can't find your wire cutters. And you will never again be faced with having to go out to buy another pair of secateurs because you can't find yours!

Hoe – The first line of defence against weeds, your hoe should be kept sharpened so you just need to skim it across the surface of the soil to chop the weeds back. This kills annual weeds but it only weakens perennials. Hoe on a dry, sunny day for maximum effect, because the weeds wilt and die on the warm soil.

A Dutch hoe is the type used with a pushing action; it looks like a small pitchfork with a blade across the bottom. A draw hoe is pulled across the ground, and is good for getting rid of tougher weeds.

Rake – A garden rake, with short stubby tines, is used for levelling soil. I also use mine to bash any left over clods of clay left on my beds. Raking backwards and forwards also helps to make a fine tilth.

Trowel and hand fork – These hand tools are great for weeding, and planting plug plants started off in pots.

Secateurs – The basic tool for pruning, cutting back and trimming stems, you can choose *anvil* secateurs, where a sharp blade cuts against a flat base, or *bypass* secateurs, which are more like scissors.

Wheelbarrow – Indispensable! I use builders' barrows because you get more in them and light, flimsy plastic barrows will tip over at the most inconvenient moment. My favourite barrow has an extra ridge of metal bolted round the top to make it even deeper – great for shovelling large quantities of manure.

Thinking about buying large equipment, such as a polytunnel? Check out IDEA 34, The undercover gardener.

Try another idea...

Sundries – Other useful items include: a *dibber* – for planting seeds (I use an old pencil); *string* – for tying things and measuring out straight lines; *labels* – whether you buy fancy copper ones, plastic 'type on' labels or just use a piece of yoghurt pot and a permanent marker, it's really important to keep a record of what you've planted; *sharpening stone* – for sharpening blades; *small knife* – I have a fireman's knife for all sorts of small cutting jobs.

TOOLS FOR CLEARING ROUGH GROUND

If you have a new allotment, or are clearing an area of field or overgrown garden, these tools are useful.

Petrol strimmer – These are expensive, but can be hired or borrowed from some allotment associations. With a brush cutter blade strimmers are ideal for cutting back high nettles, brambles and docks. Be sure to wear goggles in case you hit a stone or other debris hidden in the undergrowth and the strimmer bounces badly. You should also wear steel toecaps and a protective overall (useful if you hit any hidden dog muck – believe me, I've done it!).

'Tickle it with a hoe and it will laugh into a harvest.'
Traditional English saying

Defining idea...

99

Sickle – This is a small hand-held tool with a crescent shaped serrated blade for clearing long grassy vegetation. Hold clumps of vegetation in your left hand and draw the sickle towards you, close to the ground, with your right hand. Be careful – these are sharp.

Slasher – This looks like a hook on the end of a pole, because that's essentially what it is! Slashers do what you would expect – you slash away at overgrowth and it hacks them down.

How did it go?

Q   All these tools look really expensive. Do I have to have them all at once?

A   *No, you can start with a spade, a fork, and a pair of secateurs. Look for tools at second-hand sales. That way, you can build up your collection without spending vast amounts of money.*

Q   Is it worth buying the cheap tools you sometimes see at the garden centre or even the supermarket?

A   *While some are no doubt serviceable, you tend to get what you pay for. In the early years of gardening, I even had fork and spade handles snap as I dug our heavy soil. I have asked for tools as gifts at Christmas, and for birthdays. I also think good second-hand tools are better than cheap new ones.*

24

The best laid plans...

With adequate forethought, you will find you make fewer, potentially costly, mistakes, and that the plants you try to grow are suited to your site and soil.

Don't get carried away and buy hundreds of packets of seeds and plants only to find you haven't got the space to grow them all.

The best time to start planning your garden is late autumn so the plot is ready to be planted up in early spring. The layout of your productive garden depends on how much land is available. Try to make sure you have enough space for four beds, for crop rotation, as well as a permanent bed for fruit bushes and trees.

Make a list of all the vegetables you would like to grow on your perfect plot. You'll have far too many, but it will give you a starting point. Break the list down by making a table with thirteen columns – one for every month of the year, and a column for the names of the plants. Check in gardening books to see what months the things you want to grow will be in the ground – from sowing to harvest. Tick the appropriate columns and you will get a better idea of what you will have space to grow. You can shorten the time some things need to be in the ground by planting seed in modules for transplantation into the ground later.

Here's an idea for you... **Increase the productivity of your garden area by planting perennial fruit and vegetable plants as hedges to divide up your plot. These could include raspberries and any of the hybrid berries (such as tayberries), blackberries, 'step over' or espalier apple trees, or globe artichokes. You can be as inventive as you want.**

Once you have your list honed down to realistic proportions, it is time to buy your seed. Going through the seed catalogues is a delicious early winter occupation. But save it for the evenings, because you need the afternoons for digging!

You need to remove any weeds and, if the ground is previously unused, you need to rotovate (once the ground is weed free) or dig the patch over. Exposing the turned soil to frost – especially if it is heavy clay soil – will improve the texture and aerate the beds.

Traditionally, new ground is dug in trenches. There are a variety of methods but the simplest involves digging a trench about 30 cm wide and to the depth of your spade. The soil from this trench should be taken to the back of the bed you are digging. As you dig the next row, the soil should be put into the first trench you dug. Add rotted manure and compost to the mix. If the beds have been dug previously, they will still benefit from forking over, and the addition of organic matter and well-rotted manure.

BUILDING RAISED BEDS

Another option you should consider is building raised beds. This is particularly useful if you have thin soil, or poor drainage. Raised beds are also an idea if you want to grow plants that require specific soil conditions (such as blueberries, which need acidic soil).

The sides of beds can be built using anything convenient. I have built them with planks, scaffolding boards, and even old plastic left over from double glazing! Fill the beds with soil, compost, well-rotted manure, leaf mould – whatever you have handy.

Want to find out about getting the most out of your soil? Have a look at IDEA 27, A turn around the garden: crop rotation.

Try another idea...

RAISING PLANTS FROM SEED

You can grow a huge crop of fruit and vegetables from seed bought for very little money. These seeds will enable you to feed your family for months. Seed trays can be bought inexpensively, as can plant pots, or you may prefer to buy a propagator. These vary from simple seed trays covered by a clear plastic lid to electrically controlled contraptions that create gentle heat to give seeds a boost as they germinate. You will also need compost. It is worth buying compost specially made for seeds for a really good start. Alternatively, you can make your own by using your own compost mixed with rotted leaf mould.

Whatever you raise your seeds in, make sure you give them enough light as they grow or you will end up with long spindly seedlings – 'leggy', as gardeners call them. If you are growing your plants on a windowsill and the seedlings turn towards the light, turn them round. If at all possible, grow your seedlings in a greenhouse so they will get the all-round light they need.

'The trouble with gardening is that it does not remain an avocation. It becomes an obsession.'
PHYLLIS McGINLEY, poet

Defining idea...

How did it go?

Q **I have a relatively small garden and have to make use of all the ground I can, as well as using containers on the patio. How can I make sure I use the ground to maximum effect?**

A *It is worth planting slightly closer together if your space is limited; this is easiest if you have deep or raised beds. Make sure the soil does not become depleted as the nutrients are used up with intensive planting. Add compost and well-rotted manure to combat this. Try planting fast maturing 'catch crops' such as lettuce in between other crops to increase your yield.*

Q **I've heard that I should keep off my clay-based soil in winter. Is this the case? If it is, how can I work on the garden if I can't stand on the soil?**

A *It is true you should stay off heavy soil in particular because you will compact it with your feet and lose aeration. This is actually true all year round, but particularly so in winter, when the soil is likely to be wetter. You can get round the problem by having a wide plank to walk on. This will distribute your weight more evenly and stop the damage.*

25

Little weed!

You've found your ideal vegetable garden – except that it's waist deep in nettles, docks and thistles. Take heart: with a little time and effort, you can beat them!

Are they weeds or wildflowers? Can you use them for something or are they thuggish invaders? Know your enemy!

The first time we came to look at our smallholding, the fields were studded with wildflowers. The bottom field (still my favourite) was spangled with dog violets and spicy cowslips. Bliss! By the time the deeds were in my hand, the top field was a carpet of vetch, knapweed and drifts of harebells. Butterflies busied themselves in the fields by day, and fat, furry hawk moths fluttered by night. I thought I'd died and gone to heaven.

Unfortunately, these delicate wildflowers are not the only things that flourish in the fields as the year unfolds. Vicious weeds choke everything in their sights. Nettles send out opportunistic feelers in every direction (but at least they are a good indicator that the fields are fertile). The butterflies, of course, love them and the patches are soon festooned in silk and tiny furry caterpillars. Then there are docks that grow in many clumps. However, they come in handy with all those nettles around, and my goats love them!

Here's an idea for you...

Make weeds work for you!
Some weeds can be composted,
especially annuals such as
chickweed. Others – especially
perennials such as couch grass
and thistles – should not be,
because they can regrow in the
heap. Feed these to your
animals or put them into an
incinerator. Once they are
burned, scatter the ashes on
the compost heap and mix them
in. Steep nettles in water to
make a nourishing 'tea' for
watering plants. Some of the
fresher, tiny weeds, such as
wild rocket and dandelion, can
even be eaten in salads!

Goosegrass is another common problem. This is the plant that comes with little sticky balls that mat into dog and cat fur, and your socks. Goosegrass may be low creeping, but it sprints across open ground and can choke a strawberry patch in days. But the worst yob in the weed world that I have encountered is couch grass. This awful weed sends out runners so tough, they can punch through plastic. And every segment has tiny hair-like roots. It is terribly hard to eradicate.

If you've made the decision to garden organically, no chemicals can be used on your weeds. Alternative means of attack need to be developed. My first strike is to send in Gracie and Sweetpea – my goats. They are the advanced guards and clear the top growth, even cheerfully munching spiky Scotch thistles. Once they have done their bit, I dig over the area for the new bed. (Note: do not rotovate because that chops weeds up into small pieces. That's OK for annuals, pre-seed setting but *terrible* for perennials such as thistles, couch and bindweed because all those little chunks of root are capable of creating new plants. If only roses rooted so readily!)

I pull out all of the large sections of root and send in the second wave of troops – the hens. Scarlet, Ruby and Pinky (they *are* Rhode Island Reds…) eagerly scrabble through the soil picking out pieces of weed and they also offer the added bonus of eating the leatherjackets and wire worms that infest newly cleared grassland.

Do you want to use weeds for good? Find out how in IDEA 39, *Magical muck*.

Try another idea…

Next, I fork over the soil to remove any stubborn tap roots. That leaves the soil ready for improvement. Because we garden on heavy clay, I dig in grit and organic matter (generously supplied by Khola and Evie, our gypsy cobs) to improve drainage.

If you are planting fruit bushes or similar perennials, plant them and then cover the bare soil with a water permeable membrane. I cover the membrane with heavy mulch. Where I garden it is windy and there's lots of wildlife, so I used pea gravel because organic mulches tend to blow away, although they may work on your site.

Above all, attack weeds when they are small. This gives you a fighting chance. If you leave it because you are too busy, weeds grow large and are harder to remove. Large weeds harbour slugs and other pests. There is also the danger that the weeds will set seed and your problem will be multiplied.

'Whoever said a weed is just a wildflower in the wrong place should be tied up with bindweed and dropped into a clump of stinging nettles!'
EMILY PICKLES, author

Defining idea…

How did it go?

Q **I've seen black plastic rolls at the builders' merchants. It's a lot cheaper than mulching plastic. Can I use it?**

A *I have trialled this around fruit bushes and trees, and it does cut out light to stop the weeds in their tracks. But be sure to poke holes in it to allow water to run through. (I didn't do this first time and ended up with puddles and thirsty plants!) You can also use old carpet (people save them for me), which rots in time. I have used wet newspaper too, which worked well around my strawberries. Be sure to weight it down, though. (I didn't the first time and spent a morning fishing sheets of paper out of my hedgerows – duh!)*

Q **Can I use compost as a mulch?**

A *You can, and, indeed, as it rots it will improve your soil texture. However, use it very thickly – and that goes for all mulch designed to combat weeds. A thin covering will not block out the light and the weeds will grow through. Be careful that your compost does not contain any weeds or you could be storing up trouble for yourself.*

26

Get down and dirty

If you are trying to buy a smallholding, check out the soil before you purchase the property – both the depth and type. Without good, hearty soil, your vegetables and fruit will never thrive.

Save yourself heartache later on. Grill the vendor about the land, and take good notice of what is growing already (even if it is just weeds). Ask permission to take samples. Don't be afraid to be cheeky.

Turning over a hand trowel of soil (or, better still, a spadeful) will show how deep the soil is. If the soil depth is very shallow, you may have problems, so it is worth checking. But beyond the depth of the topsoil, how do you check what *type* of soil you are dealing with? Quite simply, test it. You need to know about your topsoil before you can think about what you can grow.

There are five main types of soil: sandy, clay, loam, chalky and peat. Sandy soil is light and easy to dig. If you pick up a handful, it will feel loose and a little gritty. In windy areas, this type of soil can even blow away! Water runs through sandy soil quickly, and nutrients can be leached out of the soil as the water drains away. All is

Place a small amount of soil, about 5 cm, in a jar. Add water to fill the jar and shake it. Leave it to settle overnight. Any gravel and coarse particles such as grit and sand will settle on the bottom. Lighter, smaller particles will form a layer on top of this and any organic matter will float on the surface. If the gravel and sand layers are the biggest, you have sandy soil. The gritty layer above this shows you how much loam is present. If the clay layer – the tiny particles – is the thickest layer, you have a clay soil.

not lost, however – a sandy soil can be improved by the addition of lots of organic matter such as compost, and well-rotted manure to make it more water retentive and bulky.

A clay soil is heavy, and can be hard to dig. When you try to dig a clay soil, it sticks to your spade, and your feet. A handful of clay soil will stick together if you add water. It will roll into a ball between your thumb and fingers. In dry spells, clay cracks and can become iron hard and inhospitable to plants; in wet spells, puddles may lay on the ground for days, drowning growth. Clay soil has very small particles, and the best way to improve this type of soil is to dig in plenty of organic material such as leaf mould and well-rotted compost, together with manure.

You can also help matters by digging in the autumn, leaving the large clods exposed to the cold weather and frost. This will help to break them down into a fine tilth. We have managed to create a rich, very productive soil here on clay using these methods. Be careful, though, not to tread on clay-based beds if you can avoid it. If the soil is compressed, the aeration is lost.

Loamy soil is dark and crumbly, and full of organic material. When you rub a handful between your fingers, it will feel smooth. Loam is great for growing most plants.

Chalky soil is pale, even to the point of looking grey. Again, water drains away quickly and you will need to dig in plenty of water retaining organic matter in the form of manure, compost and leaf mould.

If you want to enrich your soil, get some pointers in IDEA 39, *Magical muck.*

Try another idea...

Peat-based soil is confined to a few areas, but it is very fertile and water retentive, as the soil is made up from decomposed plants. However, it can be very acidic.

ALKALINE, NEUTRAL OR ACID?

The pH level of the soil can affect what will grow there. Most vegetables prefer a slightly acidic soil, with a pH of between 5 and 7 (neutral being 7). Potatoes, marrows and tomatoes like their soil slightly more acidic, at around 5 to 5.5. Brassicas prefer a slightly alkaline soil, with a pH of around 7.5.

So, it's time to get out the test tubes and indulge your mad scientist fantasies! You can buy simple pH testing kits from garden centres (both online and 'real'). You take soil samples from different parts of your garden or land and add different solutions to determine the pH balance of your soil. You match the solution colour to a supplied chart and the colour shows you the pH level of your soil samples.

'Soil is often taken for granted – treated like dirt. Although it may look lifeless, the soil is a complete underground living environment, teeming with life.'
HDRA Encyclopaedia of organic gardening

Defining idea...

113

If your soil is overly acidic, you can dig in lime to correct this. I tend to dig it in after I dig over ground to leave it to overwinter. The rain washes it through the soil, ready for spring planting. This only needs to be done every two or three years. If it is too acidic or alkaline, most plants cannot easily absorb the minerals and nutrients in the soil and they will be stunted.

How did it go?

Q   Some areas of my land are acidic, but others aren't. How can this be the case?

A   *If a field is overgrazed, it can easily become acidic. The animals crop the grass down to the roots and drop heaps of dung, which soon makes the soil acidic. The grass plants cannot break down the high acidity because they are being overgrazed.*

Q   I have been offered a large quantity of cheap mushroom compost. Could this improve my soil?

A   *Spent mushroom compost is a real boon. It improves the physical structure of the soil and increases the activity of useful micro-organisms and earthworms. It is also pleasant to work with, with an earthy smell and a crumbly texture.*

27

A turn around the garden: crop rotation

No, this doesn't mean you have to spin your carrots or turn your turnips. It just means that you don't grow the same type of crop in the same place every year.

Crop rotation reduces the chance that diseases will build up in one place, giving you sickly or diseased plants, and it stops the soil from becoming impoverished.

Permanent crops (such as fruit bushes, fruit trees, many herbs, rhubarb, asparagus, strawberries, artichokes etc.) do not need to be rotated and can be planted anywhere in the garden that pleases you. You do not need to move them.

Annual crops that you harvest, and then they are finished (such as carrots and other root vegetables, potatoes, peas, beans, leeks, onions, beetroot, cabbage and greens) are different. You should establish four beds to give you a rotation. This sounds like a fuss, but it's worth it. If you grew cabbages, sprouts and cauliflower (members of the *Brassica* family) in the same bed every year, you would run the risk of the ground

Here's an idea for you... **Use potatoes as a starter crop for any bed before you begin your rotation because the bulky leafy cover blocks the light and stops many weeds from growing. Moving potatoes from bed to bed helps to keep weeds under control.**

becoming infected with club root – a disfiguring disease that makes cabbages sickly, with, quite literally, roots like a club that cannot take in nutrients properly. If you move the bed that you use each year, you reduce the risk.

Likewise, carrots and parsnips should be moved year by year because they are susceptible to root fly. Leaving them in the same bed makes it more likely that the pests will build up to epidemic levels the next year. In the same way, onions should be moved to reduce the risk of onion fly. Rotation has been used for centuries to combat these problems.

Another important reason for crop rotation is to stop the soil from becoming impoverished by losing nutrients particularly used by a given crop. Rotation makes use of goodness in the soil left over from previous crops.

When planning your beds, it makes sense to group plants from the same family together; it also makes sense to group plants together that enjoy the same growing conditions. By grouping together plants that have the same nutritional needs, you will be able to feed the soil specifically to suit each group. Peas and beans like lime and are greedy feeders, so lime may be added to the bed. Brassicas like fairly alkaline soil, so it would make sense for them to follow the peas and beans into a bed on the next rotation.

HOW TO ORGANISE CROP ROTATION – YEAR ONE

Find out how to make the most of your garden in IDEA 24, *The best laid plans...*

Try another idea...

The most commonly used system is known as the three-bed system. The confusing thing is, it uses four beds. Basically, you divide your plot into four beds. The first bed is for your root vegetables, such as carrots, parsnips, Jerusalem artichokes, beetroot, etc. I like to add a leaf mould and plenty of comfrey 'tea' to this bed before planting. Make sure, if it's a new plot, that there are not too many stones in the soil. (But don't think you will ever remove them all – they breed! I just tell myself they are good for drainage.) Too many stones, and your root veggies will fork as they hit the stone, and grow into strange shapes.

The second bed is for brassicas: cabbages, broccoli, cauliflowers, Brussels sprouts, kale, etc. It should be fed with manure and comfrey tea as above, but I like to add a little lime to the mix the autumn before planting.

The third bed is for heavy feeders, so dig in as much manure as you can over the winter. In this bed you can plant potatoes, beans, peas, celery, sweet corn, marrows, courgettes, tomatoes, leeks and cucumbers.

The fourth bed is left to lay fallow. It is not the end of the world if you do not have room to leave a bed fallow each year; it just helps to avoid the soil becoming impoverished, and it reduces the risk of soil becoming infested with diseases.

'Gardening requires a lot of water – most of it in the form of perspiration.'
LOU ERICKSON, female baseball icon

Defining idea...

YEAR TWO AND BEYOND...

Rotate the beds so that you now grow the plants from the first bed in the second bed, the plants from the second bed in the third bed, and the plants from the third bed in what was the fallow bed, leaving what was the first bed fallow for a season. (If you do not have a fallow bed, the plants from the third bed end up in what was the first bed.) In years three and four, everything moves on a bed again in the same way. In the fifth year, everything is back where it started in year one.

How did it go?

Q I've heard that adding lime to the soil can help to prevent club root in brassicas. Is this true, and can I add lime across all of the beds?

A Lime does help to prevent club root, but I would not add it arbitrarily across the beds. When lime is added to soil, it increases the pH so the soil becomes more alkaline. Not all plants need this, and in fact some positively dislike it.

Q Why do you leave a bed fallow?

A This keeps the ground pest free and well nourished. Grow green manures such as mustard (this has the added advantage for land being converted from grass to vegetable bed in that it helps to rid the soil of root eating wire worms). A fast growing leafy crop helps to keep weeds down, but it also adds much needed organic matter to the soil when you dig it over into the soil again.

28

Vegetable matters

For many people, growing vegetables to feed their family is one of the main things they want to achieve when they downshift. There are many to choose from.

You can grow a rich variety of vegetables, including heritage vegetables that you would not be able to buy in the shops, even at a premium.

Fresh, crunchy carrots, lifted from the soil; earthy new potatoes and sugar snap peas – there is nothing like growing your own vegetables. They need a minimum of cooking and few sauces because their intense flavour is unlike any vegetables bought in the supermarkets, which will have been harvested and stored for days.

What to grow depends on your tastes, of course, and the space you have available. If you only have a small area, concentrate on things that are expensive to buy. However, there are some vegetables that should be found in most vegetable gardens.

Cabbages – Fresh spring cabbage, bursting with sweetness; curly leaved savoy, with its rich 'green' flavour – there are cabbages for all year round. Cabbages need rich, fertile ground heavy with manure. Seeds can be sown straight into the beds, or you can sow them in plug trays and transplant them outside in about five weeks.

Here's an idea for you...

Grow asparagus in well-drained beds for a delicious treat – savoured all the more when it is so expensive in the shops! Asparagus may be grown from seeds but for a quicker start buy crowns (basically roots). Keep them weed free and they will be productive for up to 20 years. The ferny fronds that grow after you stop cutting the spears (in early summer) are lovely for floral displays.

Broccoli – Broccoli is quick to grow, and has so much more flavour when grown at home. The purple sprouting variety is delicious and unusual, but just as easy to grow. Broccoli needs plenty of space, with plants growing up to a metre tall! Broccoli seems to grow best when the seeds are sown in place, but they can be grown as plugs and transplanted.

Cauliflowers – Cauliflowers can be temperamental things, prone to branching off. Keep them well watered, though, so they grow steadily and you will be rewarded with tight curds that make the most delicious cauliflower cheese you have ever tasted. Again, these will grow from seed or transplants.

Onion family – These like rich, well-manured soil. I put in more unusual varieties, such as red onions and shallots, but a good onion and leek bed will keep you in material for stews for months! You can grow onions from seed, but I grow mine from sets, which are small onions that put on growth quickly.

Carrots – Carrots grow well in lighter soils that must be kept weed free. If you want carrots without strange forks and shapes (which my family rather enjoy – especially the rude ones), dig over the bed and make a fine, stone-free tilth. Sow carrot seed sparsely, straight into the ground – the more you have to thin them out, the more chance there is of carrot root flies getting a whiff and colonising your beds.

Parsnips – Parsnips also do best in a light soil, but they can be slow to germinate so don't lose heart. Don't water parsnips too heavily or they may tend to split and become soggy. The flavour improves with frost, so dig them as you need them.

Fancy growing fruit? There are tips on how to in IDEA 29, *Get fruity!*

Try another idea...

Sweet corn – Sweet corn is an amazing crop to grow. It grows tall, up to 1.8 metres, and whispers as the wind blows through it. In fact, it can get a bit spooky if you have a large patch and you're a devotee of horror films! Sweet corn is wind pollinated and needs to be planted in blocks rather than rows so that the pollen can move from one plant to another.

Tomatoes – Strictly speaking, these are fruits, but they are generally eaten as a savoury so they are included here. Different varieties of tomatoes can be planted outdoors or in polytunnels and greenhouses. The seed should be sown indoors and the seedlings transplanted at about 15 cm tall. They are greedy feeders, so add organic fertiliser such as comfrey tea to your watering can. Home-grown tomatoes surpass the taste of any water blown varieties bought in the supermarket – even those bought on the vine at great expense. If you grow nothing else, poke some tomatoes in the conservatory.

Sweet peppers – Except in the warmest areas, these are best grown indoors. The soil should be rich and well manured, and the plants will need plenty of water. Green, orange and yellow peppers are just less ripe versions of red peppers. You will get six to eight peppers from most plants.

'In the night, the cabbages catch the moon, the leaves drip silver, the rows of cabbages are a series of little silver waterfalls in the moon.'
CARL SANDBURG, author and poet

Defining idea...

Lettuces – Lettuce grows best in light soils, with plenty of organic matter. The key is to never allow them to dry out. If lettuces are allowed to dry out, they are more likely to bolt (run to seed). Sow your lettuces in rows straight into the ground. Also, make successive sowings – i.e. sow a short row every couple of weeks to avoid a glut that needs using all at once.

How did it go?

Q   I'd like to grow pumpkins and squash. Are there any special requirements?

A   These plants, along with marrows and courgettes, only flourish in warm weather. They put on huge amounts of growth to create trailing plants that cover a large area of soil. All they need is plenty of water and ground rich with manure for a healthy crop.

Q   I don't have a huge amount of garden, but I'd like to grow potatoes. What would you recommend?

A   Don't put scarce ground down to main crop potatoes. Instead, concentrate on unusual and heritage varieties such as pink fir apple potatoes, which have a delicious nutty flavour, or 'purple Peruvian', a knobbly blue potato that's great in salads. You could also try 'Russian banana', a yellow 'fingerling' potato that has rich, waxy flesh and is beloved of gourmet French chefs. You can even grow these in large containers on the patio if space is tight.

29

Get fruity!

Fruit in jewel colours, ripened in the sun and brought straight to the table – what more could you ask for? Fruit is the crowning glory of any smallholding.

Today, with access to fruit grown around the world, we are spoiled for choice. But all too often, we get our expensive bounty home to discover there is very little taste. All those fuel miles for nothing.

So what can you grow at home? Obviously this depends on your climate, but a huge range of fruits can be grown for the table wherever you live.

Apples – Apples can be grown on all manner of rootstocks, from large standard trees to small patio trees. They are easy to grow and give a good, reliable crop. If you are planting apple trees, check whether they need a pollinating partner and plant accordingly to ensure the tree sets fruit. If you have space, plant a few crab apples too. They are great for making jelly and are full of pectin, a necessary ingredient for making jams set.

Why not grow grapes in your conservatory if you have one? Grapes can be grown outside in warmer areas and some varieties can even be grown in cooler climes if against a wall. If you are growing grapes inside, choose a large pot, or a permanent indoor bed, and add plenty of sand to the soil.

Pears – Pears need fertile soil. They can be grown as large trees or bushes. Check the rootstock to see the final size the tree will make before planning. There are self-fertile pears, but check – you may need to plant cross-pollinating varieties.

Quinces – This beautiful tree is a relative of the pear. Quinces are self-pollinating and easy to grow, and the fruits make a scrumptious jelly, or wine.

Nectarines and apricots – These trees need protection from frosts. If you live in a cold area, they may be better grown in a polytunnel or greenhouse. If the flowers appear very early, before there are pollinating insects on the wing, you have to pollinate the flowers yourself by tickling them with a soft paintbrush, transferring the pollen from one flower to another.

Peaches – Peaches need well-drained soil. If you live in a cool climate, they are best trained against a wall for shelter as they are prone to frost damage. If they flower early, be prepared to pollinate them with your paintbrush.

Cherries – You can grow dessert cherries – sweet ones for eating – or more acidic cherries for bottling. You can buy dwarf varieties, but a standard cherry is a splendid sight if you have the room – and a mature tree can yield an amazing 35 kg of cherries!

Plums, damsons and greengages – These trees need deep, rich soil but give a great return. A mature standard plum tree can give you 25 kg of fruit. The blossoms may need protection from frost, but otherwise these are easy to grow and productive trees.

Strawberries – Strawberries like well-manured soil. They are easy to grow and give a good crop, obligingly sending out runners that can be potted up to make new plants. Once the strawberries have formed, and are ripening, protect them from birds with fleece. I also use bottle cloches to keep slugs at bay. Straw is sometimes put under ripening strawberries, but it can harbour slugs. Old carpet tiles are a cheap and effective alternative.

Raspberries – Raspberries are a great fruit to plant, even if you have limited space. They give a heavy yield, and can be trained up wires strung between posts, to make a garden screen. After the canes have fruited they should be cut down to the ground because the fruit is formed on year-old canes.

Blackcurrants – Blackcurrants need rich soil. Enrich the soil with manure or compost when you plant them. They will grow in semi-shade or full sun, and prefer well-drained soil. Mature bushes can grow large, so leave about 1.5 metres around the plants. Blackcurrants fruit on year-old stems, so cut out old stems after they have fruited to encourage new fruiting growth.

Want to grow vegetables? Find out how in IDEA 28, *Vegetable matters*.

Try another idea...

'*If you want to be happy for a short time, get drunk; happy for a long time, fall in love; happy for ever, take up gardening.*'
ARTHUR SMITH, *radio presenter*

Defining idea...

White and redcurrants – White and redcurrants are variants of the same species. They fruit on old wood, so there is no need to prune. Although they do not fruit as heavily as blackcurrants, they produce enough to make a welcome addition to summer puddings and redcurrants make wonderful jelly.

Gooseberries – Gooseberries are easy to grow and give a good crop once they are mature. The bushes will crop for up to twenty years. They need well-drained soil but it must retain moisture. There are many varieties of gooseberries, including sweet red dessert berries and berries for cooking.

Blackberries – Cultivated blackberries are generally larger and sweeter than their hedgerow counterparts. They should be planted in manure-enriched soil and trained along wires fixed to a wall or strung between two posts. After they have fruited, old canes can be cut down to the ground.

Loganberries and tayberries – These hybrid berries should be treated like blackberries. They look like large, rather dark raspberries and are very sweet. They prefer slightly acidic soil and can be trained up a wall or on wires.

Q   **I'd love to have a go at growing melons – is it feasible in a cool climate?**

A   *Melons can be grown under glass, in a greenhouse or in a polytunnel. They make large and trailing plants that grow four to five melons per plant. They need rich soil full of organic matter, and must be kept well watered.*

Q   **I planted some blueberries in the garden but they look rather sickly. What am I doing wrong?**

A   *Blueberries like highly acidic soil, and it is unlikely you have this in your garden. Dig up the plants and put them in a container full of ericaceous (for acid-loving plants) compost. Feed the plants with potash as berries are forming.*

How did it go?

129

30

Self-contained

Even a tiny garden – or an apartment with a yard – can be used to grow edible produce if you know what containers to use.

Containers can be used to grow a wide variety of tasty crops, so don't be put off by thinking you haven't got enough space — start cultivating!

Containers are a convenient way to grow many tender and specialised plants. If you have limited space, container growing is a must. No space is too small to grow food. It can be grown wherever sunlight penetrates. You can grow plants in pots on windowsills, in conservatories, on balconies, in windowed stairwells and in roof gardens. If you live in an urban area this is even more important, because you need to build yourself a green oasis of calm that you can slip into to slough off the stresses of the day along with the grey grime of city living.

You have to be inventive and adaptable to make the most of your limited area. Use all of your vertical spaces, by fixing trellises for growing peas and beans – they don't need much floor space. Use hanging baskets for herbs and tumbling cherry tomatoes. And build window boxes for herbs and salad plants.

Here's an idea for you...

Make your own 'growbags'. Even though the commercial varieties are cheap, they are of variable quality and may not be organic. Fill strong rubble sacks (from a builders' merchant) with your own home-made compost, worm casts, rotted manure and leaf mould mixed with a little soil. Seal the end with duct tape – it's waterproof and strong. Lay the 'growbag' on its side in its final position and use a craft knife to make a slit or window in the side. Then plant your tomatoes, cucumbers or whatever you fancy.

The great thing about container gardening is that you can start small, adding to your collection whenever you are ready. Try to grow a small amount of a wide variety of crops until you find what works, and what your family enjoys.

CONTAINERS

You can use anything that will contain compost. Old plastic catering-size food containers are ideal and available very cheaply – look in classified ads for details. Avoid non-food containers in case they have been filled with anything toxic.

Recycled sinks – not just the expensive antique variety, gorgeous though they are – together with old dustbins and tyre piles can make fabulous yard containers. They are big enough for you to grow fruit trees. Basically, anything that is big enough for the plant you want to grow is fine. Look at growth charts to work this out. Use your imagination – family and friends will likely have containers they are finished with that will be useful too.

Wooden troughs are easy to build from rough wood and can be painted to add rustic charm. These can contain anything from salads to climbers such as peas and beans. Recycled plastic containers can be bought cheaply from gardening centres and they are light enough for use on a balcony or in a roof garden. Baskets lined with polythene are also useful and light, and they are decorative too. If you use clay or pottery pots, make sure they are frost resistant if you intend leaving them outside during the winter.

Be sure to clean containers thoroughly to make sure you do not transfer any diseases from year to year.

Find out more about growing in smaller spaces in IDEA 14, *Self-sufficient in suburbia: garden farming.*

Try another idea...

COMPOST

If it is humanly possible, have a compost bin. These are often available at a subsidised rate from your local council, so check it out. Worms are also a great addition to your compost making efforts. You can buy special kits or alternatively you can buy brandling worms (*Eisenia foetida*) from a fishing supplies store and add them to a container yourself. You can use any container with a tap at the bottom – adapting old wine-making equipment works well. The tap allows you to drain the liquid (essentially, worm pee) from the bottom of the container. This makes a great feeder to spray on plant leaves. Dilute 1:20 with water and put it in a spray mister.

The container needs a shelf inside for the worms – a piece of wire mesh works well. The worms have to be kept out of liquid they produce or they will drown. Add about 1.5 to 2

'There are no gardening mistakes, only experiments.'
JANET KILBURN PHILLIPS, gardener

Defining idea...

kg (dry weight) of shredded newspaper to the bin after it has been moistened with water. Then add the worms. Give them kitchen waste to feed on and remember they aren't keen on citrus or spicy foods. Add shredded newspaper as necessary to stop the container becoming anaerobic and smelly. Keep a lid on the top to exclude flies.

The worm bin should be totally emptied twice a year, after leaving it for a fortnight without adding any new material. The worms will wriggle to the top, and are easily removed to a temporary pot whilst you remove the rich matter left in the bin. You then start again with fresh newspaper.

How did it go?

Q   **I'm worried about the wind catching the containers and destroying my work. What can I do?**

A   *Anchor them securely, and be careful about where you stand them – give them protection from structures such as walls and sheds. If you use larger pots, these are less likely to be a problem in wind. You can, however, stand containers together and lash them together with cord to resist wind damage. Containers can be bolted down with L-shaped brackets but this rather takes away the portable nature of container gardening.*

Q   **What grows well in a container?**

A   *Most edible plants! Salads, tomatoes, strawberries, potatoes, peppers, herbs – if you fancy growing a vegetable or fruit in a container, give it a try and you will probably be successful.*

31
Food for free

Canny downshifters don't eat just the fruits of their smallholding. They hunt all over for the bounties of nature – the ancient ancestors of the cultivated plants we eat today.

Hedgerows, meadows and streams even today yield a wide variety of food and useful plants for the informed collector – just make sure you know what you are picking!

Marsh samphire, blewits, ramsons, pepper dulse – the sensual indulgence of these foods can be heard as you breathe their names. I have been a fan of wild food since I nibbled shiny red 'bread and butter' – or hawthorn berries, to you – on the Sussex Downs as a child, their sweet-potato flavour bridging the gap from the early afternoon until dinnertime.

Obviously, you have to be careful that the food you gather is the food you think it is – and not just with gathered fungi. Studying field guides and attending the proliferation of courses run by local wildlife organisations are great ways to avoid mistakes. You also have to be careful that the food you gather is not near to a road,

Here's an idea for you... **If you are a little worried about collecting wild food, grow some on your own patch. I love wild strawberries, with their tiny sweet fruits. I have grown a patch from seed and they now merrily romp in the shade of my willows. I also grow wild rocket because I like to gather it in large quantities. And I grow violets and primroses specially (I don't gather wild ones, which is undesirable and prohibited) so I can crystallise them for sweets.**

and thus tainted with lead from traffic. Ensure, too, it comes from an area untouched by agricultural chemicals. You should never uproot the plants, and only take small quantities of leaves, etc. from any one specimen.

Even bearing these warnings in mind, the fun that can be had – and the flavours to be discovered – make a foray for wild food a rewarding and pleasurable activity. Coming home with a basket of wild food ready for the kitchen makes me feel in touch with my pagan forebears who stepped on the earth lightly, and were rewarded for their stewardship with an overflowing wild store cupboard.

IN THE WOODS

Sweet chestnuts, with their spiky, silky cases, are a great source of protein – and can be gathered in parks as well as woodlands. Take them home and roast them – roast chestnuts are a delicious winter tradition. They are also lovely candied (poached in sugar syrup) or made into a purée, which is a tasty and protein-rich pie filling when mixed with onion and mushrooms.

Fungi may be gathered and eaten, so long as you are very careful about identification. There are over 100 types of edible mushroom in the UK, including chanterelles, blewits, oyster mushrooms and ceps. There are also a few poisonous varieties; some fatally so, such as the amanitas. Although I have been on organized fungus forays and enjoyed the delicious 'fry up' at the end, I only gather the mushrooms *Agaricus campestris* – field mushrooms – that grow in my fields as a result of all the horse dung that accumulates there.

> **Learn how to make preserves from your free bounty in IDEA 33, *Hitting the bottle*.**
>
> *Try another idea...*

AT THE BEACH

Many types of seaweed are edible, including carragheen, dulse, kelp and filmy green sea lettuce. Perhaps the most famous is laver, the type eaten as a delicacy in parts of south-western Wales and Japan. In Wales it is made into a purée and sold in cakes called laverbread, which are often fried.

IN THE HEDGEROWS

Hazelnuts fresh from the hedgerow are a delight. Careful as you pick them, though, because they grow in small clusters and are easily shaken to the ground, to be lost for ever in the inevitable tangle of briar and nettles growing below.

> **'On the motionless branches of some trees, autumn berries hung like clusters of coral beads, as in those fabled orchards where the fruits were jewels...'**
> CHARLES DICKENS
>
> *Defining idea...*

Wild rowan berries (*Sorbus aucuparia*) can be gathered to make into tart jelly, as can vitamin C laden rose hips.

IN THE MEADOWS

My absolute favourite 'meadow food' is wood sorrel (*Oxalis acetosella*), with its shamrock-shaped, emerald green leaves. It tastes sharp and fresh in a salad, and has been eaten in this way (and in sauces) for centuries. Apparently, the food police decree that you should not consume too much because it contains oxalates (salts that it is not good to consume in large quantities) but a little of what you fancy, as they say, does you good.

Fat hen (*Chenopodium album*) is another great wild vegetable – and not just for the name. It is one of the first plants to colonise ground disturbed by road building, new housing estates, etc. It has been used as a food since Neolithic times and is largely eaten in the same way as spinach. It is loaded with iron, having more than Popeye's favourite.

Q **We have loads of wild roses in the hedgerows. My mother says she used to give us rose hip syrup as kids for the vitamin C. Is it worth making?**   *How did it go?*

A *Rose hip syrup has been made for centuries. During WWII the syrup was made in huge quantities while citrus fruits were not available. Wild rose hips contain four times the amount of vitamin C found in blackcurrants, and twenty times the amount found in oranges! Make the syrup by boiling topped and tailed hips in water and straining the liquid through muslin before reducing it down by simmering, being careful not to let any hairs from the seeds inside the hips remain as they are a stomach irritant.*

Q **I've heard you should 'pull' mushrooms rather than cut them. Is this true?**

A *Yes – you need the whole stalk and any 'sheath' for accurate identification. Gently twist, rather than yank, and you won't damage the plant either.*

32

Good companions

Planning a garden is like making a seating plan for a dinner party – you have to be careful about what you put together to make sure they get on.

Many plants work in harmony with their 'bed mates' to boost growth and ward off pests. Successful home farmers tend to work with Mother Nature, using her own weapons in the war against pests and diseases, and maximising growth.

The principle behind companion planting is to grow plants together in combinations that benefit the plants so they grow better than they would have done if grown singly. Of course, a general diversity of plants – rather than few varieties – also helps to minimise the effects of pests and diseases.

Firstly, you should look at the way the plants you are planting benefit each other in terms of shelter and the creation of microclimates. We live in a very windy site and I have planted a shelter-belt of trees and shrubs to give my plants a chance. I have started dividing parts of a field with shrubs to make separate areas for fruit bushes

Here's an idea for you...

Take a 'leaf' out of the book of the indigenous people of South America. Plant sweet corn, runner beans and outdoor cucumbers together in the same hole. They call this 'the three sisters.' The sweet corn grows tall and protects the plants below it from wind and sun scorch. The runner beans grow upwards, round the tall woody sweetcorn, and don't need wigwam support. The beans offer dappled shade, and the cucumbers grow rampantly across the shady ground.

etc., thickening hedgerows with native species and thick spiny *Rosa rugosa* which have wonderful jewel bright hips in the winter.

You can also use taller plants to shade more tender plants from the heat of the sun. Beans and peas, for example, grown up a willow wigwam, can shield tender leafy lettuces that may suffer in strong sunshine. The leaf canopy gives dappled shade and helps to prevent possible scorching.

BAD COMPANY...

There are a few examples of plants that don't like each other's company for one reason or another. Tomatoes growing next to potatoes is a bad idea – they come from the same family (*Solanum*) and, amazing as it seems, cross-pollination is possible. Both crops are at risk of blight, so it makes sense to keep them apart to reduce the risk of both crops being infected, should blight strike.

...AND GOOD INFLUENCES!

Tagetes (the frilly looking French marigolds) have been suggested as having a limiting effect on bindweed and couch grass. I am currently trialling this in my own vegetable garden. Since tagetes also guards against whitefly, I gain anyway – even if the couch grass is undeterred. Tagetes smell strongly, and help to hide the smell of cabbage leaves from cabbage white butterflies looking to find a handy hatching site for their hungry caterpillars. The butterflies 'taste' with their feet, and if they land on several unsuitable plants in a row, they will fly off – but if they land on several suitable plants, they will stop to lay eggs.

Discover about creatures that can help you in IDEA 36, *Animal allies.*

Try another idea...

Marigolds also seem to discourage eelworms (the type that give you a nasty surprise when you cut open a potato) and this is thought to be due to a secretion the roots give off as they grow.

Carrot fly can be fooled by planting onions and French marigolds. The stinky onions – and marigolds – mask the carrotty smell, so the flies blunder off in search of carrot patches anew. I do this, and have never suffered from carrot fly infestation. Could be a coincidence, but I'll carry on, following the 'if it ain't broke, don't fix it' principle. These fabulous flowers also attract hoverflies – the beneficial insects that are stripy, like a flatter bodied, darker looking wasp. Hoverfly larvae feed on aphids, so they are a real friend to gardeners – especially of the organic persuasion.

Borage helps to attract aphids, keeping them away from broad beans. As it is also a great beneficial insect attractor, with gorgeous blue flowers that go very well in a jug of Pimms, I'd say it was worth a try.

I have many apple trees and am about to plant a new orchard. I am keen to try organic scab protection and remedies, so I shall be planting garlic and chives underneath. The bonus is, I get to use (and give away) loads of garlic – and I should stay safe from vampire infestation!

'We need good companions to help us to flourish in this garden we call life.'
SOPHIE HUDSON, philosopher

Defining idea...

Chives are invaluable in the kitchen, and I always want more than I grow. The flowers are beautiful, and once again attract pollinating insects.

I start off loads of tobacco flowers (nicotiana) every year – they smell great and make a lovely cut flower. They have a kind of sweet sticky substance on the stems that attracts whitefly, and so draws them away from other vulnerable plants.

How did it go?

Q **I have trouble with woolly aphids on my fruit trees. Can I plant anything to help deter them?**

A *Nasturtiums can do this job rather well. Just plant them around the base of the tree and allow them to grow up it. It may be that the plant secretes a substance that is taken up by the roots of the tree and repels the woolly aphids. Apart from looking good, nasturtium leaves make a great, peppery addition to a salad.*

Q **I've heard that French beans are useful companions for any brassicas. Why should this be the case?**

A *Apart from physical support – the tall beans sheltering the growing brassicas – the beans fix nitrogen from the air, and the soil is enriched. Brassicas are hungry feeders, and benefit from the surplus nitrogen the beans produce.*

33

Hitting the bottle

Ruby red raspberry jelly, glowing blackberry jam, squash and red onion chutney, and peaches poached in brandy – preserves are the jewels of the downshifter's winter store cupboard.

With a few jars and a sturdy pan, you can bottle the essence of summer. Opening a jar and breathing in the fragrances transports you back to warmer days – and reminds you why you downshifted in the first place.

Bottling fruit – You can bottle fruit the innocent way – or the boozy way. Fresh fruit can be bottled in sugar syrup. Add about 225 g of sugar to 600 ml of water and stir it over a medium heat until the sugar dissolves. Bring the solution to the boil. Pack clean, trimmed fruit into a wet sterilized jar (boil them in water to sterilize them) and pour the syrup over the fruit. Tap the jar on the table to allow air bubbles to rise to the surface, and seal the lid. Keep the bottled fruit in the fridge.

Boozy bottled fruit lasts longer, and makes a lovely dessert with ice cream and meringues. Pack fruit such as raspberries, strawberries or currants tightly into a sterilized jar, and pour in cheap generic alcohol until the fruit is submerged. (Gin or

Here's an idea for you... **Make herb vinegars and oils with the bounty from your herb garden. Simply add sprigs of washed herbs to sterilised bottles and pour in oil (olive oil works well) or white wine vinegar. The bottles look pretty stood in the window and the warmth of the sun helps the flavours to infuse. Use the oils and vinegars in salads and cooking.**

vodka works very well, with the added bonus that the colour of the fruit totally infuses the alcohol; peaches go well with brandy.) Seal the lid, and this lasts for years, with the pungency of the fruit essence growing stronger over time.

Jam – Cook your fruit in a large, heavy-bottomed pan. With raspberries and strawberries, as well as other soft fruits, simmer the fruit until it looks pulpy and mushy. Add sugar (special jam sugar can be bought from the supermarket). The amount you add depends on the type and amount of fruit you are using. Keep the jam simmering, but do not let it boil because it burns easily and tastes dreadful. To test for 'setting point' you can use a thermometer, or drop a blob of jam on a cold saucer – if the blob forms a skin you can wrinkle and push with your forefinger, it has reached setting point. If not, return the jam to the heat for a little longer.

When the jam reaches setting point, leave it to stand for 15 minutes. Then pour it into warm, sterilized jars. Cover the top of the jam with circles of waxed paper and seal the top with a lid or cellophane. It's worth decorating the jars if you are thinking about selling your jam. You should label the jam with the date it was made, and the ingredients.

Jelly can be made in the same way as jam, but the fruit pulp is sieved out, which seems a bit of a waste!

Chutney – Chutney is just savoury jam. I take my chosen vegetables (whatever is bountiful in the garden at the time, which makes for some odd mixtures but experimenting will help you find the tastes and textures you like) and simmer them in cider vinegar until the vegetables are tender when poked with a knife. Add soft brown sugar and simmer the mixture for about an hour until it thickens. The amount of sugar and vinegar you need depends on the type and quantity of vegetables you are using. Ladle the hot chutney into sterilized jars, then seal and label them.

If you want to cook and freeze your produce, check out IDEA 21, Frozen assets.

Try another idea...

Pickles – You can pickle some vegetables, such as onions or cabbage, without cooking them. Others, such as beetroot, need to be boiled before pickling to give them a palatable texture.

'I feel a recipe is only a theme, which an intelligent cook can play each time with a variation.'
MADAME BENOIT

Defining idea...

Prepare your vinegar – the pickling medium – well before you are ready to pickle your vegetables. I add my chosen spices to warmed vinegar, which I then put back into the jar for up to a month so the flavours infuse well. Slice and cook your chosen vegetables, and pack them into sterilized jars. Fill the jar with vinegar until the vegetables are submerged, and add a little more. Seal the lid. The vinegar is highly acidic and bacteria will not grow in such inhospitable conditions.

147

Fruit curds – Curds are easy to make and are a great way of using up excess eggs. They can be made with any citrus fruits, including oranges, limes, mandarins, kumquats, etc.

Grate the rind of three or four large fruits (obviously more if using smaller fruits). Squeeze the fruit and collect the juice. Put 120 g butter, 900 g sugar, the juice and grated rind into a pan. Heat the mixture until the butter melts and the sugar dissolves. Beat four eggs in a ceramic or metal bowl. Place the bowl in a pan containing boiling water to a depth of about 4 cm. Add the juice mixture to the eggs and mix well. When the mixture thickens, remove it from the heat and put it in sterilised jars. Keep curd in the fridge because it doesn't last too long.

How did it go?

Q   Do I need to add pectin [setting agent] to jam?

A   *It's up to you and your recipe – be prepared to experiment. Some fruits are high in pectin, such as crab apples. I often add a couple of these, made into purée, to my mix. Preserving sugar sometimes contains pectin, which will do the job.*

Q   How do I pickle eggs?

A   *Simple: put fresh hardboiled eggs in a sterilised jar, cover them with spiced vinegar, and seal. You can start to eat them after about a month.*

34

The undercover gardener

Providing plants with shelter from harsh weather allows you to extend the season and grow more tender crops. Bring on the 'polytunnel'!

Polytunnels can be moved to different parts of your land, and offer a large covered growing area at a relatively low cost — so what are you waiting for?

I got a polytunnel for my fortieth birthday. For some women it's diamonds; for me, this was a long-held dream come true! If you live in a cool climate, a polytunnel allows you to grow many things you could not grow outside, such as aubergines, peppers, okra, and melons. The protection a polytunnel offers lengthens the season, and allows things to ripen, such as tomatoes, that may not ripen outside in colder regions unless the summer has been a good one.

In addition, polytunnels can provide a winter growing season. This can allow you to grow some of your favourite crops all year round. Heat loss from a polytunnel is greater than through a greenhouse, but with the correct choice of crops you will be able to grow through the winter.

Here's an idea for you...

If you are buying a second-hand tunnel, do all you can to ensure you get to help to dismantle it. This gives you a good idea of how the pieces go back together. If you don't help to take it apart, you may find yourself with a puzzle you can't put back together!

Once you have decided to buy a polytunnel, you have the 'adventure' of erecting the beast to look forward to. Choose a flattish site, preferably in a sheltered area. Think about the services you might need, such as water and electricity. You can manage without electricity but having no water is much more of a problem. You will have to water daily, especially in hot weather. Soaker hoses pegged to the ground are one option. If you are not near a water supply, don't forget you can also use water butts to collect water for use in your tunnel. Incidentally, keeping water inside the tunnel is a good idea, particularly if you are watering seedlings. Water that is too cold can 'shock' your plants.

Many suppliers now offer the option of heavier duty covers for exposed and windy areas. The first thing to do is to erect the hoops, digging them into the ground and adding cement to the holes on exposed sites. Then add 'hotspot tape' to the hoops to prolong the life of your cover. There are two ways to secure the cover to the framework. You can either bury the edges of the covering in a trench, or attach them to a wooden side rail. If you are burying the cover, make sure it is well secured in the earth. The strength of your polytunnel depends on how well you fix the cover to the ground.

There are various grades of cover for you to choose from. Go for the best you can afford. A standard polythene cover lets about 90% of the light through. Other grades are heavier; some let more light through. If you are undecided, go for standard polythene. Your cover will need to be replaced every five to seven years, and if you want to try something different at a later date, you will have the opportunity.

Want to know more about growing food in containers? Find extra tips in IDEA 30, *Self-contained.*

Try another idea…

Enlist the help of a friend to erect your tunnel hoops – and another for adding the cover. Don't try to put the cover on when it is windy, or it may tear and you may end up airborne! Adding the cover on a hot day is a good idea because the heat of the sun will soften the plastic and this will help to strain it into a tight fit.

You will also have to think about doors. Check that the door you choose is wide enough to get a wheelbarrow through, or you will find life gets rather difficult. Ventilation is another consideration – in summer, temperatures can easily exceed 100°F. Apart from leaving the doors open, you can spray water on the inside of your polytunnel to reduce the temperature. You can also provide additional shade by growing shade plants (I grow grape vines).

Once your polytunnel is erected, weed control becomes an issue. As soon as the cover is on, the weeds will shoot away. I have covered the floor of my tunnel with black weed-control membrane, because the field where it is situated is very weedy.

You can plant straight into the ground. I have planted nectarines and peaches straight into the soil, knowing they will be protected from the extremes of the weather. You can also grow plants in pots or raised beds.

'The thankful receiver bears a plentiful harvest.'
WILLIAM BLAKE

Defining idea…

How did
it go?

Q   **What sort of maintenance is required for a polytunnel?**

A   *Not much. Algae may have grown on the plastic during the course of the growing season, so it will need a yearly clean. Washing-up liquid and a mop will do the job, with a hose for rinsing. Any holes can be repaired with special kits available from the tunnel manufacturer. Small holes can be repaired with polytunnel tape.*

Q   **I am going to plant lots of my crops into raised beds and the soil already in the polytunnel. How can I make sure I maintain soil fertility?**

A   *The same principles you use in the garden will work in the polytunnel. Add organic matter to the soil, such as leaf mould, rotted seaweed, and home-made compost. You should also consider a crop rotation system in your beds. This need not be complex; ensuring that you do not grow any crop in the same bed two years running should be enough. Don't forget to use home-made feeds such as nettle or comfrey 'tea' for your plants.*

35

Free and easy

Propagation is easy and the equipment you need is cheap and readily available. Go ahead, get new plants for free.

You can sow seed — which is free if you save your own — or you can take cuttings to increase your plant stock.

Vegetative propagation – making new plants from parts of growing plants (for example, taking cuttings) – is an easy way of freely obtaining new plants. This type of propagation gives you clones; plants identical to the parent plant. New plants grown from seeds are more variable.

TAKING CUTTINGS

This simple technique allows you to create new plants to replace plants that are becoming woody and past their best. It is a good way to produce young plants to make a hedge of lavender, box, or rosemary cheaply. You can take cuttings without harming the parent plant as long as you are careful and many cuttings can be taken from a single plant.

Don't worry if you do not have a greenhouse – cuttings can be grown easily on windowsills. All you need is the correct temperature and light levels for cuttings to grow successfully.

Here's an idea for you... **Make new plants from conservatory and house plants, such as African violets (*Saintpaulia*) and Cape primrose (*Streptocarpus*). Take whole-leaf cuttings from African violet, planting the stem in gritty soil. They root quickly. With *Streptocarpus* you take slices of the long leaves, cut widthways. Insert the cut edges into gritty compost, and tiny plantlets appear along the veins of the cut edges. These soon grow into strong young plants and can be sold along with herbs, etc. at local sales or markets to raise money.**

You can take cuttings for most plants, including perennials (and the tender perennials we grow as bedding plants). When you take cuttings, try to take them in the morning before the sun has much heat in it, so the plants are turgid and full of water. A wilting plant will not allow you to take successful cuttings.

As you collect the cuttings, put them in water or a plastic bag to conserve moisture. Take them inside as soon as possible and insert them in cuttings compost, several cuttings round the edge of the pot. Be careful not to allow them to touch. You can insert the bottom of the cuttings in rooting hormone (available from garden centres) first if you prefer, but many cuttings will root even without the hormone.

After you've put the cuttings in the compost, water them well but use a fine rose or a spray bottle because you do not want them to become waterlogged, or for the water spray to dislodge them.

Once the cuttings have rooted you need to harden them off. That means you need to get the plants accustomed to being outside in cooler conditions. Firstly, pot the cuttings up. Remove them gently from the pot and tease the roots out so you have separate plants. Pot them in plant pots filled with multi-purpose compost. If you have a cold frame, the cuttings can be put inside to shelter them from the worst of the weather as they become established.

Learn how to improve your soil for free in IDEA 39, *Magical muck*.

Try another idea...

SAVING SEED

You can save the seeds from 'dry seeded' plants such as beans, peas, poppies and brassicas very easily. Wait for the seeds to mature on the plant if possible, then snip the heads over a paper bag (not plastic because any moisture will be trapped and cause the seeds to rot).

If you fear a long bout of rain as the seed pods or heads are coming to maturity, snip them a little early and hang them up in a dry, well-ventilated place. Once they are dry, again store them in paper.

Seeds from pulpy fruits, such as tomatoes, have to be dealt with differently. You can squash tomato pulp on kitchen tissue and wait for it to dry out before collecting the seeds in a labelled paper envelope – the labelling is important so you know what variety you have saved, and the date you saved it.

You can also pulp tomatoes and mix the pulp in a jar with a little water. Leave it to ferment, then scrape off the mouldy layer that forms. Drain and rinse the seeds with cold water and dry them quickly before storing them in paper.

'You aren't wealthy until you have something money can't buy.'
GARTH BROOKS

Defining idea...

155

Keep your seeds dry and cool to preserve them for as long as possible. Never keep seeds in a greenhouse or polytunnel because the heat will damage them.

The best thing I ever did, seed wise, was to join the HDRA (Henry Doubleday Research Association) seed library. Apart from helping to conserve old heritage varieties with your membership dues, joining gives you access to the seed handout once a year when saved seed is distributed. I have some excellent heritage varieties that cannot be bought in the shops from this scheme, and now save my own seed. You can, of course, swap seeds with other gardeners and become a 'seed guardian' where you grow heritage varieties for the purpose of saving pure-bred seeds for the library.

How did it go?

Q   I'd like to start saving vegetable seeds. To get me going, are there any which are really easy and have a high success rate?

A   *Many are easy, so try whatever you like. It's all trial and error! Particularly easy, though, are beans, peas, tomatoes, rocket, nasturtium and coriander.*

Q   I've saved some seeds, but how long should I expect them to last and still be viable?

A   *If you store seeds in the correct conditions – cool and dry – they can last a long time. Even after many years, some may make new plants. However, as a general guide, long-lasting seeds (more than five years) include pumpkin, artichoke, borage, cucumber, squash and chicory. Cabbage, cauliflower, lettuce, tomato and sunflower seeds last up to five years and carrots, onions, peas, sweetcorn, leek and parsnip last roughly three years.*

36

Animal allies

It is true that bugs can do harm in the garden but if you garden organically you'll be on the way to befriending *beneficial* insects and they'll help you to rid the garden of pests.

Quite apart from the possible health problems that chemicals can cause for humans, they can kill more of the helpful, highly mobile predatory insects than the true pests.

One of the reasons many people grow their own food is because they want to feed their families on organic produce. They know pesticides can do more harm than good in the garden. Chemicals kill off the food supply the beneficial insects need to survive – namely, the undesirables. While this is a good thing in the short term, it means the predators will move on or die off as their food disappears. As soon as there is a new infestation – and there will be – there will be no predators left and you are committed to spray even more chemicals to kill the pests.

Avoiding pesticides will help to build up the population of beneficial insects that will help to manage and dispatch the pests in your garden.

Make a small pond with a stone pile next to it to encourage predators. The pond and general dampness will entice frogs, toads and newts to the garden – good news because they eat slugs and snails. The creatures do not live in the pond, but they will shelter in the damp area around it. The pond is required for their aquatic young.

HELPFUL INSECTS AND HOW TO ENCOURAGE THEM

Ladybirds – Perhaps the best-known 'gardener's friend' is the red coated ladybird. Her larvae, looking like a tiny Dr Who monster made from tyre treads, eats even more aphids than the parent, so look out for them. You can encourage ladybirds by leaving matted grass at the base of hedges, or make a ladybird motel with a wood frame filled with the hollow stems from cow parsley or Queen Anne's Lace. These creatures hibernate.

Lacewings – These pretty little lime green bugs with crystal wings and flicking antennae are also fearsome aphid predators, despite looking like fairies. They also like somewhere to overwinter in the same way as ladybirds.

Ground beetles – These shiny black beetles are fabulous creatures – they eat the eggs and young of slugs and snails. They can be encouraged by mulching thickly around plants, because that's where the beetles like to overwinter.

Hoverflies – The larval stage of the hoverfly – the stripy but strangely flat-bodied flying insect – feed voraciously on sap-sucking aphids. To encourage the adults, plant nectar rich flowers, such as poached egg plants, between your fruit and vegetables. The adults feed on nectar and will obligingly litter the area with their young.

Centipedes – These are the long, rusty red creatures you see scuttling about in the leaf mould. Don't mix them up with millipedes – the similar but more cylindrical, black bugs – they are vegetarians. Centipedes are hunters, and will dispatch slugs, and slug eggs.

Parasitic wasps – Parasitic wasps come in many shapes and sizes, and many insect species have parasitic wasps specific to them as hosts. The adult female wasps lay their eggs in other insects and the larvae develop as parasites, killing the host.

Harvestmen – Harvestmen look like spiders, but have one body segment. They eat caterpillars, slugs, aphids and other pests. They live in grass and undergrowth so an area of the garden left wild will encourage these useful creatures.

Fancy keeping your own bees? Look at IDEA 37, *More honey for your money.*

Try another idea...

OTHER TYPES OF WILDLIFE ALLIES

Don't forget the humble hedgehog. On hot summer nights, this prickly predator can be heard crunching slugs and snails with disgusting relish in suburban gardens and country smallholdings alike. You can encourage hedgehogs by building log piles and by leaving piles of dry leaves at the foot of hedges. Don't forget to check bonfires before you light them in case a wayward hog has taken refuge for the night.

'Gardeners, I think, dream bigger dreams than Emperors.'
MARY CANTWELL, author and previous editor of *Vogue*

Defining idea...

Encourage birds to live in your garden because many species eat your pest enemies. Feed the birds during the winter, and put water out for them. Leave out collections of nesting materials in spring, such as animal hair clippings, hay or wool. You can also introduce nest boxes.

You can, of course, also remove pests by handpicking them from plants (I regularly make guerrilla sweeps of the garden at night with a torch and a 'slug bucket') or setting traps such as the ubiquitous beer trap for slugs. These can also be filled with a mixture of milk and oatmeal. Strangely enough, grapefruit skins are also great slug attractants and they can be left on beds overnight and disposed of in the morning. Old carpet tiles also create a haven for slugs that hide in the dark and can be removed in the morning.

How did it go?

Q **Should I encourage birds or try to scare them off? Are they helpers or will they just munch all of my berries?**

A *Different types of birds eat different food. Pigeons will attack seedlings, and can make mincemeat out of unnetted soft fruit. However, a single blue tit raising a brood of young will gather up to 15,000 caterpillars in a season – and that's good news for your brassicas. I prefer to plant extra fruit, and cover only the most precious with fleece (never netting as birds can tangle in it and be damaged).*

Q **Is it worth buying predatory insects as 'biological control' from gardening suppliers? They seem expensive.**

A *It may be worth buying them for a 'captive area' such as a greenhouse or polytunnel. Buying them for a large area outside would not really be cost effective. I like to encourage the creatures I find already, but if I never saw ladybirds in my garden I would be tempted to buy a couple of packets of young to release and hopefully create a breeding colony.*

37

More honey for your money

Bees are fabulous for the smallholder – drowsy but industrious, they remind us of ourselves! They also have the added benefit of providing honey and wax.

Got a problem? Had a major life event such as a birth, death or marriage? As tradition has it, you should go and tell it to the bees so it's handy if you've got some!

Before sugar cane became accessible to the developed world, honey was the sole source of sweetener. It's cheap to produce and is very saleable if you need to boost your income as a downshifter.

Before you even consider buying your own hives and colonies, join a beekeeping group and get experience. They are very friendly and will be able to steer you in the right direction when you are ready to buy your own equipment. Some groups sell off their old equipment too.

You need a bee-proof outfit, boots, a beekeeping hat with a face protector and gloves. Using a smoker before handling the hive or the bees is a sensible safety precaution – the bees don't like the smoke, but rather than making them angry it makes them react by filling their honey sacs, which in turn makes them bloated

Don't forget that the wax is as valuable as the honey, so collect it. The wax is the cappings cut off the honeycombs. It can be made into wonderful fragrant polish and the best, sweetest smelling candles in the world. Melted with a gentle heat, you can add herbs, such as lavender flowers, to make the wax even more fragrant.

and sleepy. They are easy to remove from the frames then with a soft brush.

Your hive doesn't need to be a beautiful antique affair; bees are happy in a plainer home! It needs to have a waterproof roof, and a narrow slit for bees to enter the hive. It has a brood chamber, filled with frames for the bees to build the combs. Above the brood chamber are 'supers' – the boards removed to obtain honey. There is also a frame called a queen excluder, which comes between the brood chamber and the supers. 'Clearer boards' are used for separating bees and honey. These are placed between the brood chamber and the supers, and they have a one-way system – the bees can enter the brood chamber but can't get back into the supers. Within twenty-four hours, most of the bees will be clear of the supers – the part you remove to obtain the honey.

Put your hive or hives in a sheltered position, away from strong winds, and near to sources of nectar and pollen, such as a herb garden or patch of wildflowers. Placing a hive in your orchard or near your fruit bushes and trees has the added benefit of ensuring the bees pollinate your blossoms too.

WHO'S IN THE HIVE?

In a colony of bees in a hive, there will probably be between forty and sixty thousand bees. There is, as every child can tell you, only one queen. She lays the eggs to maintain the colony. There are also a few hundred drones. These are male bees and exist to fertilise the queen. The thousands of worker bees collect the pollen and nectar. They are undeveloped female bees. When they are newly hatched, they feed the queen and the grubs, and help foraging bees unload their booty. After about fourteen to twenty-one days, they begin to work outside the hive, carrying water, pollen and nectar. They also clean the hive, removing dead bees, debris and faeces.

Do you want to start a business selling your honey? Find help in IDEA 10, *Getting down to business*.

Try another idea...

THE BEEKEEPING YEAR

In early spring, the queen bee starts to lay eggs. You should feed her with sugar syrup as natural food supplies will be low. Nectar and pollen plants are scarce, but you can think about planting food plants with catkins and early flowers especially for your bees to visit at this time of year. In late spring bees start to fly on warm and sunny days. They collect nectar and pollen from blossoms such as hawthorn, apple and plum trees.

By early summer, pollen and nectar supplies are high, and the queen is laying many eggs. By late summer, honey is ready to harvest. Remember to leave at least 16 kg of honey in the hive for the winter. You can remove between 9 and 18 kg per hive if you harvest your honey once a year. After the harvest, the bees will clean the nest, and you should start feeding sugar syrup or candy (icing sugar and water) for the bees to build up winter reserves.

**'A swarm of bees in May is worth a load of hay
A swarm of bees in June is worth a silver spoon.'**
Traditional saying

Defining idea...

167

How did it go?

Q **Now I have a hive, I'd quite like to have a go at making mead. What do I need to do?**

A   *Mead – the sweet wine made from honey – was one of the first alcoholic drinks, and was used during pagan ceremonies. Making mead is similar to making wine. Make a honey solution (1.4 kilos honey : 4 litres of water) by boiling the water and adding the honey to the water as it cools. Pour the mixture into a demijohn and add wine-making yeast, lemon juice and citric acid (this aids fermentation; it can be bought in chemists'). Fix an air lock and leave the mead to ferment for about two to three weeks. Siphon off any sediment, and put the mead into sterilised bottles. It may take three years for mead to be at its best!*

Q **I'd like to plant some nectar rich plants for my bees. Which types are best?**

A   *Try to make sure you have nectar and pollen rich plants all year round, from catkins in early spring to a border full in summer. Open flowers, like poached egg plants, are the best because they give easy access to bees. These plants, among others, are very attractive to bees: alfalfa, red clover, purple horse mint, agastache, borage, lemon balm, monarda, honeysuckle, foxglove, aquilegia, comfrey, vetch, lavender, cotoneaster, lupin and sage.*

38

Chicken run

Keeping hens is a delight. For very little effort, they repay you with eggs that taste better than any others you'll have eaten before, including free range.

Because you are getting the eggs fresh from the hen — and you know what she's eaten and how she lives — the golden-yolked beauties she gives you are without compare.

It is simple to get started with hens. Even a suburban garden can support a trio of hens – but don't buy a cockerel unless you want to be bombarded with complaints! Hens do not need a cockerel to lay eggs – you only need a cockerel if you want eggs to be fertile, for hatching.

Hens need secure housing. Whether in the country or in suburbia, foxes prowl daily, looking for unwary poultry. It is nice to see hens range freely, but I have seen too much carnage to allow that now, when foxes are sliding by during daylight whenever the fancy takes them. Instead, fence off an area and place the henhouse inside it. The hens have freedom, but are protected from predators. The fencing needs to be 3 m high, with around 10–15 cm of the mesh buried in the ground to foil a burrowing predator.

When you are clearing a bed after cropping, or establishing a new bed, give your hens access and they will clear the ground of green weeds and bugs such as slugs and wire worms. I have a simple timber frame, with chicken wire round the sides, that is the same size as my beds. I let the girls loose for a few hours and they help clear the ground while fertilising it at the same time.

The henhouse itself can be anything from a shed with a closable pop hole (hen exit) and run, to a triangular purpose-built arc. Your hens need somewhere to lay their eggs, and somewhere to roost. You need to have easy access to the eggs without disturbing the hens. Specially made hen sheds are available which have doors on the nesting boxes for egg collection.

You must provide your hens with bedding. (Ours like wood shavings best, but also lay in boxes lined with hay or shredded paper.) They need to be cleaned out regularly, and the bedding changed frequently to avoid an infestation with mites. Hens also need water on demand. We have a metal water dish but you can buy all manner of automatic troughs if you prefer.

Hens need grain, which you can buy cheaply in sacks from agricultural suppliers, or markets. This can be scattered on the ground for the hens to peck, but I prefer a metal hopper strung from the roof of the run. This is like a tube with a dish attached to the bottom. There is a gap in the tube, which you fill with grain. As the hens eat the grain, more drops from the full tube and refills the dish.

Hens also eat kitchen scraps and garden waste, and love fresh greens such as cabbage or kale. You can also offer your hens layer's meal or pellets. Hens that have access to ground in which to scratch are happy hens – they do not really need extra grit. If your hens are more confined, offer them ground shell grit. It helps if you can move hens around to scratch at different parts of the garden from time to time because keeping them in one place for too long can lead to a build up of parasites. Hens also like an area where they can scratch in the dirt to give themselves dust baths. Apart from keeping them happy, it helps them to rid themselves of parasites.

Would you be interested in keeping other livestock? If so, check out IDEA 40, *Animal instincts.*

Try another idea...

Make sure you have everything ready for your hens before they arrive; it is easy to get carried away and have anxious hens waiting to get out of boxes as you are trying to assemble their shed.

We have had everything from recovering ex-battery hens to beautiful but tiny bantams and silkies. What you choose is up to you.

Hens – *Rhode Island Reds* are a good choice; they are a traditional breed and quite hardy. They lay beautiful brown eggs. *Light Sussex* is another hardy and attractive traditional breed. They lay large browny/buff eggs. *Marans* are beautiful, stripy birds that lay large speckled dark brown eggs (but not in huge numbers). The Light Sussex/Rhode Island Red cross is also popular. They lay well, and have the added benefit that their chicks are white if they are male, and reddish if they are female. If you are raising your own chicks from eggs, that is very useful – it can be downright impossible to sex chicks and very young hens.

'To fulfill a dream, to be allowed to sweat over lonely labour, to be given a chance to create, is the meat and potatoes of life. The money is the gravy.'
BETTE DAVIS

Defining idea...

Bantams – These are smaller than hens, and lay correspondingly smaller eggs – kids love them. My favourites are *Old English Game.* These look like a child's drawing of a hen, and the cockerels are hysterical – very fiery natured, but the size of a large crow!

 How did it go?

Q **My hens have stopped laying. I know it's winter, but does the weather affect them to that extent?**

A *Hens don't like extreme temperatures, certainly – but it is light levels and the falling number of daylight hours as winter approaches that stops hens from laying. It seems an expensive nuisance to keep feeding hens through the winter when no eggs are laid, but the arrival of the first egg in the coop is a real herald of spring!*

Q **I've kept hens for a while now and I fancy branching out into something a bit different. Where can I buy rare-breed poultry?**

A *Look for classified advertisements in magazines such as* The Kitchen Gardener *and* Country Smallholding. *A great and knowledgeable supplier is The Wernlas Collection (check out wernlas.com).*

39

Magical muck

Soil can easily become depleted if you do not nurture it carefully. Making your own compost is the best way to create fertility without recourse to chemicals.

Soil is the engine of your garden. Without rich soil, your attempt to grow food will end in failure.

Making compost harnesses nature's own cycle of growth and decay. It takes unwanted vegetable matter and rots it down into rich, friable soil enhancer. Making compost can be virtually free. You can build your own containers as simple boxes by nailing together old pallets, planks or wood off-cuts. Build two, next to each other, so that once you have filled the first one, and it is rotting down, you can be filling the second one.

You can put a wide variety of things on the compost heap to get it started. Add annual weeds, but avoid the seed heads as they will be spread along with your compost. Add grass clippings (not too much at once or they can make your compost heap slimy and smelly), vegetable and fruit peelings, tea leaves and used teabags, and crushed egg shells. The key to making good compost is to use a mixture of ingredients. Young 'greens', such as grass clippings, need to be mixed with tougher, older materials such as straw. Once you have been composting for a while, you will

If you are lucky enough to have piles of leaves from trees in your garden, don't add them to the compost heap. Instead, make a wooden frame and attach chicken wire to create a mesh box. Add your leaves and leave them to break down into leaf mould. This is incredibly rich and fine, and can be used for mixes to grow cuttings and seeds.

learn to recognise if you have added too many 'greens' – making the heap slimy and wet – and add 'browns', such as hay and straw, to rectify the situation. Very dry items, such as straw, can be watered (I use nettle or comfrey 'tea') a little to encourage them to rot down.

You can add torn up newspapers in small quantities, but shred them and mix them in well. You can also add wood shavings, such as bedding from small pets' cages. This will help to keep the heap aerated and ensure it doesn't get too smelly. Straw has the same sort of effect. You can also add cotton and wool clothing, chopped up into small pieces. Don't put too much of one type of material in at once, and mix your heap well.

You can add torn up card and paper packaging to your heap too. This 'high fibre' technique, developed by The Centre for Alternative Technology in Wales, is particularly useful for smaller scale gardeners who may not have access to plenty of 'brown' materials such as straw and hay.

There are some materials that are not suitable for composting. Don't add the roots of perennial weeds such as dandelions, nettles and thistles or they will regenerate faster than Captain Scarlet and take over your garden. You can put these in a black sack together with some grass clippings and tie the top. Once they are dead – and be warned, this can take up to a year! – they can be added to the heap.

Don't add diseased plants, such as brassicas with club root or tomatoes and potatoes affected by blight, or you will spread problems around the garden.

Interested in reuse and recycling? Read IDEA 45, *What a load of rubbish!*, for tips.

Try another idea...

Don't add cooked food and meat products or you may attract rats. If you are adding woody stems and materials such as rose and shrub prunings, shred them well and mix them in.

When your compost heap has reached about 30 cm in depth, you can add a thin layer of farm manure or soil. This helps to activate the compost by adding micro-organisms and helps to keep in the heat, which speeds up the rotting process. Urine (especially male urine!) also acts as an activator. So boys – get busy!

When you add the manure, tread the heap down to get rid of large air pockets. Cover the heap with the lid if you have a bin, or a piece of old carpet if you have built your own. This keeps it warm and stops rain from saturating the heap. Rain can stop the rotting process and leach out the goodness. Turn your compost heap regularly with a garden fork so that the material on the outside, which does not rot easily, is moved to the inside to break down.

When your compost bin is full, top it off with a layer of soil – and wait. Start filling your second bin. After about three months a well-made compost heap will have broken down into rich crumbly compost that is ready to use.

You are of the same decaying organic matter as everyone else, and we are all part of the same compost pile.
CHUCK PALAHNIUK, *Fight Club*

Defining idea...

How did it go?

Q **I have a small garden, so I don't really have room for a composting area. What can I do?**

A *Composting doesn't have to be carried out on a large scale. You can buy a plastic compost making bin, often at a subsidised rate from your local council, and tuck it away behind a trellis screen along with your regular bin. It seems a shame to fill landfill sites with vegetable waste when you can quickly turn it into nutrient-rich soil improver!*

Q **I've heard about vermiculture – making special soil feed using worms to break down waste. Should I add worms directly to my compost heap?**

A *No – set up a separate bin for your worms, with a tap at the bottom to harvest the liquid they produce (worm wee, essentially) which is a rich foliar feeder. The worms are kept out of the liquid with wire mesh, and vegetable waste is added to feed them. Insulate the worm bin in winter, or move it into a shed to stop the worms from freezing.*

40

Animal instincts

If you have a smallholding, you might be toying with the idea of keeping livestock. Think carefully before you embark on what could be a long-term commitment.

An idyllic picture in your mind's eye of fields full of gambolling lambs and a cow in the meadow won't cut it.

I have two goats, two ponies, three rabbits, six cats and two dogs. I also have hens, geese and doves. They are all pets. That may fill the heart of hardcore downshifters with contempt, but frankly I don't care. I know why I have my animals – they are companions with fringe benefits. The ponies and goats are great lawnmowers, the cats catch the armies of rodents that threaten my crops, the dogs chase foxes and the hens and geese lay eggs. The doves and rabbits? Well, they look pretty, and that's enough. We are vegetarians – anathema to many smallholders!

Before you decide to keep livestock, ask yourself why – what will the purpose of the animals be? Animals are a huge commitment in terms of time, housing, vet fees, feed, etc., so you need to be sure. If your animals are pets – fine. With fringe benefits? Even better. But before you buy animals as an investment for your smallholding, consider how you will feel when you have to kill them, or send animals you have reared to be slaughtered. If this is fine with you, go ahead. I have

Here's an idea for you...

Before you buy any large animals, such as cows and sheep, go on an animal husbandry course to get a taste of what you are letting yourself in for. Many agricultural colleges run these, as well as general smallholding courses.

more respect for people who kill the animals they eat than for those who buy sanitised packages from the supermarket.

WHICH ANIMALS?

Chickens – Without a few hens, at least, it's hard to imagine a self-sufficient garden. They're very little trouble, with wonderful eggs in return, and they have few disadvantages, apart from needing to be kept safe from foxes and locked up at night. They do sometimes become infected with mites but you can treat this yourself with powder. You have to feed them daily, collect eggs, and clean their shelter regularly.

If you are going to kill hens for meat, you need to buy specialist equipment – rather horrifically called a 'dispatcher' – or learn to wring necks.

Ducks – Besides giving lovely eggs, ducks also help to mow the grass! You should have water available for healthy, happy birds. Don't expect a lovely ornamental pond: they poo a lot and munch all the weeds! Ducks need protection from foxes, too, and don't like extreme temperatures. Again, they need to be fed daily, eggs collected and regular cleaning.

Ducks can also be eaten but you will need to be able to wring their necks.

Rabbits – Rabbits are easy, cheap and pleasant to keep. They need protection from foxes, vermin and draughts. They need food and water daily, and you need to watch out for diseases. They can catch colds, get mites in their ears and they're also susceptible to myxomatosis, especially when there is a large wild rabbit population.

Learn how to fence in your enclosures in IDEA 42, *Fencing: on guard or* en garde?*

Try another idea...

Unless they are kept as pets like ours, you have to be willing and able to kill your rabbits humanely (harder than it sounds) before skinning and boning them.

Goats – Goats are real characters and are suited to most climates, although they need protection from very bad weather. They are providers of meat, milk and fleeces – some are more valuable than others. They have to be well confined or tethered or they will lay waste to your vegetable garden! They are great grazers, however, and dispatch everything from nettles to docks as well as grass. Goats need access to high levels of minerals, but this can be easily sorted out by buying 'goat licks' (blocks of salt they can, strangely enough, lick).

If you decide to keep goats for milking, be prepared to milk them every day. Make sure you know what you are going to do with the strongly flavoured milk. If you keep goats for meat they will need to be slaughtered professionally.

Sheep – Sheep are great for cropping grass and maintaining pastures, but they wander very ably. They produce meat, fleece and even milk. They are very hardy but can develop an alarming number of ailments requiring veterinary attention. When they are lambing, they need close attention. They also need their feet trimming from time to time, which can be difficult to do!

Work is either fun or drudgery. It depends on your attitude. I like fun.
COLLEEN C. BARRETT, president, SW Airlines

Defining idea...

Pigs – Pigs are cheap to feed and are fine, intelligent animals. (How people slaughter them is a mystery to me: when they do, they enjoy sausages, bacon and ham.) Pigs need feeding and cleaning out regularly, and can be hard to catch if they get loose! They are generally hardy, healthy animals with few problems.

Cows – Gentle and beautiful, cows provide milk, meat and leather. They self-feed on grass for part of the year, but need feeding regularly in winter, when they also need shelter from winds and rain. They are large animals, and you need some strength and determination to make them go where you want them to!

How did it go?

Q   I'm thinking about keeping animals for milk. Are there any drawbacks?

A   *If you are milking goats, sheep or cows, be prepared for the commitment: it needs to be done every day. Milking them takes a knack, too, but it's not difficult to learn. You do need to be scrupulous about hygiene and think ahead about what you are going to do with the milk.*

Q   What happens to my animals if I go on holiday?

A   *This causes complications, but isn't insurmountable. You may be able to get a house-sitter, as we do – neighbours or sensible friends who enjoy a free holiday in the country in return for a few feeding and mucking out duties.*

41

Hedging your bets

Hedges are the backbone of any smallholding. Planting them gives your garden structure and definition, and it's an investment for the future.

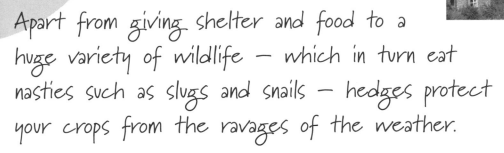

Apart from giving shelter and food to a huge variety of wildlife — which in turn eat nasties such as slugs and snails — hedges protect your crops from the ravages of the weather.

Hedging shelters crops and livestock. Farmers have known this for centuries – and if you are lucky, you may have inherited an old hedge, full of history. For most of us, we inherit no hedges at all – they were grubbed out when fields were enlarged for modern agriculture and large machinery, or they never existed to begin with. At best we may have a few forlorn hawthorns in a straggly arrangement that suggests a hedge may have existed – once.

A good hedge needs to be dense and have no gaps. It will feature the occasional full-size tree for shelter from the elements. It is very hard to make a hedge completely stock proof. Sheep in particular will find the smallest of gaps and weasel through, only to bleat pathetically when they cannot get back to the flock. I choose to

Here's an idea for you...

Buy your whips for hedges and coppices in bulk. The price gets cheaper the more you buy. If you buy fifty, you'll get a 30% discount on the price per plant that you'd pay if you bought just one. That rises to almost 50% if you buy 250 or more. These savings soon add up and as every thrifty downshifter knows, a penny saved is a penny you don't have to earn.

confine any stock with fencing, stepped inside the hedge if necessary. Some folks prefer to lay hedges so they become dense and stockproof. I run few animals so it is not worth my while – only you will know what you need.

I have inherited hawthorn hedges with great gaps at the feet where they have not been laid for many years (chopped partially through and left with a 'hinge', before bending the sapling sideways and fixing it with stakes and hethers). I have chosen to thicken these with extra planting of wild roses, blackthorn, elder and guelder rose saplings. This increases the biodiversity of the hedge – and it looks good to see a more diverse range of species rather than a hawthorn monoculture.

I have planted many new hedges. In the fields, I mainly use hawthorn or blackthorn interspersed with field maple, and native broadleaf species such as willow, bird cherry, oak and alder. As you are planting your new hedge, include some of these to grow into large trees within the general structure of the hedge. You should also consider adding wild roses, blackberries, blackthorn, elder, holly and nuts, such as hazel, which will give you extra crops to use or sell.

Hawthorn is not called 'quickthorn' for nothing. It earns its name by growing quickly, with no nonsense and no special care beyond keeping the base weed free as it establishes. It offers a froth of headily scented blossom in late spring and clusters of glittering berries, beloved by birds, in the winter. The thorns offer an impenetrable hedge if it is laid; if left unlaid, it is still quite hard to get through – whether by animal invaders or undesirable human visitors.

Hedging, fencing or both? Before you decide, check out IDEA 42, *Fencing: on guard or en garde?*

Try another idea...

You can buy hawthorn 'whips' – small saplings, supplied bare rooted, usually in their first year – for pennies from the many hedging suppliers or in bundles from farm sales and auctions. They are quick to plant, too. Make a slit with your spade, and push the whip into the split before treading the soil down to firm the whip in place. After watering, the job is done. (Holes need to be dug for larger saplings.) The small whips establish very quickly. Plant your whips in a line about 40 cm apart, but plant two staggered rows. That makes the hedge thick as the plants bush out.

I have also been experimenting with willow hedges in recent years. These grow quickly and also give me a crop – withies (willow branches) can be cut to weave into structures such as tunnels, teepees and 'fedges' (living willow hedges). I have even woven a small igloo-summerhouse for tea breaks! Within a few years, you can cut willow and sell it as rooted cuttings and withies, giving you another source of income. This may be possible where you garden, especially if you have a waterlogged or damp area, and is worth considering given the sharp rise in interest in wildlife gardening and naturalistic garden designs.

'Love your neighbour; yet don't pull down your hedge.'
BENJAMIN FRANKLIN

Defining idea...

How did
it go?

Q **Can I use leylandii for hedging? I know it gets bad press, but that's because it grows so fast. Surely that's a bonus for downshifters?**

A *Never, ever use leylandii or similar for a hedge where livestock are present – or can escape to become present! They are highly poisonous to animals. It is also not a good species for wildlife. However, that having been said, I have planted a few lines out of the reach of animals to shelter my polytunnel and greenhouses. This is in the orchard field where I grow fruit and vegetables, and the only animals allowed in are my hens (in a pen), and my tribe of itinerant felines.*

Q **I am wondering about how much space to allow between my new hawthorn hedge and my vegetable beds. How much space will the hedge take up?**

A *This is an important point. Hedges, once mature, can take up a huge amount of space. Physically, a mature single-row hawthorn hedge can be around 2 m wide. A two-row, staggered hedge can be up to 3 m wide. As well as the physical space the hedge actually occupies, you have to think about the shade it casts and the amount of nutrients and water a mature hedge will extract from the soil.*

42

Fencing: on guard or *en garde?*

Fences are vitally important for downshifters – not just because they delineate the edges of your property, but also because they keep livestock safe from going AWOL.

Fences must be strong — not like the flimsy garden fences in urban gardens. They've got to withstand high gales and the inevitable rubbing they get from the itchy backsides of your beasts.

A fence is only as strong as the gateposts, corner posts and fenceposts the wire strains against. You need to dig the holes for the posts quite deeply. With gateposts this can mean a metre deep, and even more on light soils. This gives you room to bury enough of the post, and allows you to secure it in the hole with stones, hardcore or concrete.

My first foray into fencing was dismal. Despite the 'fencing party' of assembled friends and family, the work was hard and we tried to do too much, too fast. Consequently, the fence posts did not go in deep enough and the wire was not properly strained. It quickly became a saggy mess which in the end had to be taken back down.

Adapt fencing techniques to make smaller enclosures for hens, rabbits or other small animals. Use chicken wire (buried in the ground at the bottom to foil foxes) to complete the fence, and add a couple of arks inside for your trios of birds. They can be allowed to roam within the enclosure during the day and shut up at night.

It is best to approach fencing slowly and surely. Do a little at a time and *never* fence in a rush – that is, do not buy stock until you have safely fenced your fields. Start with buying posts. They do not have to be the finely finished, dressed wood posts that cost an arm and a leg from garden centres – it would cost thousands! Hardcore or concrete is needed for fixing the posts in place, and a tool (I use a long iron bar) for tamping the material into the hole.

You will also need an auger (a type of 'earth drill') or a 'spit' – the old-fashioned digging tool used by 'navvies', which looks like a spade but has a narrower and longer, and slightly more curved, blade. The spit works well on clay soil for digging deep, narrow holes for posts. Other requirements include a post driver (a metal tube with one end capped off, and two handles), a pair of pliers, a hammer and a vaster number of fencing staples than you could possibly imagine!

If you are making a wire fence, you'll need a pair of hide gloves, a wire strainer and a spinning jenny (for unwinding wire onto in manageable lengths). If you are making post and rail fencing, you need galvanized nails and the wooden rails to fix to your posts. You also need a long steel tape measure and a spirit level.

Measure out the area you need to be fenced carefully – don't just rely on your eye; measure it out with a tape. Your posts should be around 2–3 m apart. Corner posts have to be particularly strongly set in the ground. Dig your hole, and remove all the loose soil. Drive the post into the ground with your post driver by putting the sleeve of the post driver over the post and lifting and dropping the driver to punch the post into the

If you want to make a living willow fence, find out how in IDEA 43, *Wonderful willow.*

Try another idea...

ground. Put rocks and hardcore into the hole in layers and tamp it down hard as each layer is put into the hole. If you have lots of money, you can use concrete to fill the holes too – the type especially made for posts, which you put in dry and 'water'. For lots of posts this is too expensive, but it is effective. Fix braces (smaller posts wedged against the bottom of the post) to help to strengthen the corner post further.

Continue in this way (without the braces) for each post needed. Gateposts need to be extra strong, so use heavy posts – we sometimes use sections of telegraph pole, which can be bought cheaply. It is important to ensure that your gateposts are at the same height, and level, so that you can hang the gate. Attach the gate (second-hand gates can be bought from sales and auctions, but you could make your own) with firmly driven home hinge pins. Make sure the gate opens *into* the field so it's harder for stock to escape.

You can add wire (or posts) according to the stock you are keeping. Tensioned wire, dispensed by a spinning jenny and tightened with a strainer, is fine for horses. You'll need more substantial – and higher – wire for goats. (We use heavy-duty pig wire.) Chicken wire 'does what it says on the tin' and is great for hen enclosures, but is good for other small animals such as rabbits, ducks, quails, etc.

'If the grass on the other side of the fence appears greener, it must be all the fertilizer they are using.'
KEVIN RODOWICZ

Defining idea...

How did
it go? **Q   I've seen the price of fenceposts at the garden centre – please tell me there's a cheaper way!**

A   *I buy mine, along with bundles of wire, from auctions at the local agricultural market – look it up in your phone directory or get hold of specialist magazines for farmers and look for advertisements in the classified section. I have also bought posts (or, rather, rough wood) from the local sawmills, which is a very cheap option.*

Q   Why do I need a spinning jenny? Can't I use the wire straight off the roll?

A   *Only if you want to get hopelessly tangled. I did this. Only once. The spinning jenny allows you to use the wire without it unwinding and getting kinked and tangled. That stuff is dangerous!*

43

Wonderful willow

Willow is one of nature's finest gifts to the crafty downshifter. A useful material employed since at least as early as the time of the ancient Egyptians, it is invaluable today.

As well as sustaining a huge variety of wildlife, which makes it environmentally friendly, willow can be coppiced and fed to goats as winter fodder, and it can be made into a huge variety of useful goods to use or sell.

Willow grows as if by magic. If you cut a piece of willow as thick as a pencil in the early spring, and stick the cut end in the ground, it grows – it's as easy as that. Cut pieces about 30 cm long, stand them in a jar of water or vase, and watch the little white, worm roots form in days. (Once the willow is cut, it must be stored in water to stay alive.)

Once you have your cuttings, establish a willow bed or hedge. The willow grows so quickly that once the cuttings become established plants it does not matter if you cut withies from them on a yearly basis. Plant your cuttings in a well-prepared bed, kept free from weeds or through a water-permeable weed membrane. The cuttings

Here's an idea for you...

Make a simple pixie seat – once you've made one you'll want a whole ring! Push 60 cm uprights 10 cm into the soil in a circle with the circumference you fancy for the finished seat. Weave pliable willow whips in and out of the uprights as though you were weaving a basket, keeping a fairly tight weave. Remember to push the cut end into the soil or it will not grow. Line the willow case with weed membrane and fill it to the brim with compost. Tamp it down hard with your fist. Sprinkle a bag of grass seed (plus the seed of a creeping herb such as chamomile for a lovely fragrance as you sit down) on the soil and water the whole structure. Keep it watered as it establishes, and clip the grass and herb 'seat' as necessary.

should be planted in late winter to spring, before the plants are in active growth. Protect them from browsing animals, such as deer and rabbits, until they are established. This can be achieved by cutting a piece of chicken wire and bending it into a cloche shape before placing it over the top of the cuttings.

When planting cuttings, or making a living structure that involves pushing the rods into the ground, make a diagonal cut at the bottom to make a more pointed end. If the ground is hard, use a metal spike to make a pilot hole to get you started. Thicker rods need to be planted in a hole. If you are making a structure, dig a trench and backfill it with the soil you have dug out before planting your rods.

Be warned: fast hybrids can grow up to four metres in a year, as many people buying sweet little ornamental willows have found when growth has started from the rootstock at the base of the plant!

A word of warning about location: willow roots will naturally seek water, so plant them away from water drainage systems. Be careful to plant them away from your house, too, because they can suck a huge amount of moisture out of the soil and cause shrinkage that can destabilise foundations, especially on a clay soil.

If you grow ornamental varieties, such as some of the purple or orange varieties, be sure to plant them in full sun because the colour of the bark tends to be stronger. Willow will not grow at all in deep shade, so be careful to think about the shade cast by other trees on your site – easy to forget as you are planting your cuttings before the trees are covered in leaves!

Check out IDEA 44, *Bodge It! Green woodworking*, to find out about planting coppices and using green wood.

Try another idea...

WHAT CAN I MAKE?

You can make anything from standard woven baskets or border edging – using pliable but non-living willow – to living structures such as turf topped pixie seats, living hedges (or 'fedges'), right through to sylvan summer houses.

Different sizes of rod are needed for different structures. One-year rods are very pliable and useful for weaving, whereas thicker rods are used for creating fedges and larger structures.

A 'fedge' is the name given to a living willow screen, which is halfway between a fence and a hedge. Sometimes, these are made with non-living support rods, made from chestnut or hazel, but I prefer to use thicker willow rods. The rods are pushed into the ground at regular intervals, and thinner rods are woven diagonally across the uprights to make a criss-cross diamond pattern. The rods can be tied in place if necessary with pliable willow. Once this starts to shoot, it makes a pretty living screen.

'The willow hangs with sheltering grace, And benediction o'er their sod, And Nature, hushed, assures the soul they rest in God.'
CRAMMOND KENNEDY, lawyer

Defining idea...

191

How did
it go?

Q   How can I make a wigwam?

A   *Use the same principle as for the fedge. Dig a circular trench and plant ten two-year rods of around 2 m length in the trench. Push the rods about 30 cm into the ground, about 20 cm apart. Tie the top with a fine, pliable willow rod or use a piece of cut down tyre inner tube. They are flexible and 'grow' with the willow. Plant one-year rods as diagonals and weave them onto the uprights. As the willow grows and shoots, you can either weave the material into the structure or prune it out. In the first year especially, you may like to plant other plants in the trench for extra 'cover' for your den. A good annual to choose would be sweet peas; a fragrant perennial choice would be honeysuckle, which can also be woven into the structure as it grows.*

Q   Can you suggest anything I can read to learn more about willow structures?

A   *John Warnes' book* Living Willow Sculpture *(Search Press, ISBN 0-85532-834-7) is a good place to start.*

44

Bodge it! Green woodworking

For the smallholder, green woodworking offers the opportunity to make useful items for a fraction of what they'd cost to buy new. You can even grow your own raw materials.

Green woodworking, or 'bodging', involves working with freshly cut timber to make a wide variety of goods from chairs to wattle fences and hurdles.

For thousands of years, woodlands have been used as a source of wood for creating useful things and for making into charcoal. Broadleaved woodland was coppiced, which meant regularly cutting trees down to near ground level. Coppicing rejuvenates the tree, which sends out new shoots that grow from each tree 'stool' to be cut at the next 'harvest'. This had added benefits for woodland plants, such as primroses – they could colonize the glades that sunlight could now penetrate.

Here's an idea for you...

Make a willow bed and future coppice cheaply and quickly with cuttings. Before leaf-break in the spring, cut willow wands that are about 30 cm long and the diameter of a pencil. Stand them in a vase or bucket of water. Within a week, small white rootlets form and you have rooted cuttings ready to plant. Save the willow water, too – it's great for watering newly planted trees, shrubs, cuttings and bedding plants because it contains indolebutyric acid, which is used in commercial rooting preparations.

Coppicing is not destructive, like the felling of forests. Coppicing ensured the survival of woodlands because the woodland had an economic value. In old woodland, stools can be centuries old. These stumps may be remainders of the old wildwood that existed in Britain until at least Tudor times, covering large swathes of the countryside.

For the smallholder, coppicing is an ideal craft because it only requires inexpensive hand tools to do the work and it produces material that can be used for a wide variety of tasks and products.

In recent years, a new generation of green woodworkers has revived coppicing as they have needed materials for their craft. Wood is turned and carved, and used *au naturelle* with the bark left on to make attractive rustic furniture, baskets, etc.

You can go on courses to learn the rudiments of green woodworking or bodging. These are available for everyone, from beginner to expert, starting with very simple tasks, such as selecting, cutting and splitting wood, and progressing to the use of the various tools. Ten years ago, Maurice Pyle (mpwoodsmith.co.uk) the first green woodworker I'd met, came to our school and we all had a go at working with a pole-lathe – I was hooked. A short course will teach you how to make a manual pole-lathe, and you can take it away for working on your own projects. It is an ancient technique used to turn green wood without any of the dangers associated with mechanical methods.

The recent rise in interest in garden design has increased the demand for green woodworking products, such as split hurdle fences, gates, pergolas and furniture. Locally produced barbecue fuel – charcoal to you and I – has also become popular. If you learn to make these things, this will enable you to make a very profitable product to sell and supplement your income.

Want to go on other countryside related courses? Read through IDEA 16, *Look before you leap: finding out more*, for inspiration.

Try another idea...

If you have fields, it is worth planting trees that make useful coppice plants. Plant willow – in many colours and varieties – because these may be cut very soon after planting (within two to three years). Hazel, oak, poplars, lime, and ash are all trees that can be used as a sustainable crop. You can buy trees as 'whips' very cheaply in bundles from hedging suppliers. These are small trees but grow quickly as long as they are kept weed free and are protected from vermin and deer. Use chicken wire to fence around the area planted, or protect each tree with a proprietary plastic strip. They are easy to plant – I make a slit with a spade and poke the root into the hole before closing it again with my foot.

A coppice on your land will look beautiful, especially if underplanted with woodland flowers. It will create a new habitat for beneficial insects, small mammals and birds. Just as important, though, is the fact that for a small outlay in cash terms, it will give you a sustainable source of fuel and materials for creating useful objects – a downshifter's dream!

'Knowing trees, I understand the meaning of patience. Knowing grass, I can appreciate persistence.'
HAL BORLAND, US author

Defining idea...

How did
it go?

Q   What sort of tools should I buy to coppice and bodge?

A   *You need very few, actually, and can add to them over time as you see what you need. A billhook is a useful blade with a hooked end that is useful for pulling branches towards you and cutting. You may also need a good strong chopping axe and a hatchet for general cutting as well as closer work. You may also need knives for whittling and chisels for shaping. An adze may be useful (similar to an axe but with a blade at right angles to the handle) and the back of the head may be another similar blade, a pick or a hammer head. Don't forget you can make your own pole-lathe on a course, or you can buy one from many of the green woodworking businesses you can find online. With the pole-lathe you can create all manner of turned items from chair legs and spokes to spoons.*

Q   How long will it take for my newly planted willow coppice to grow?

A   *A coppice planted with one-year whips will take some time to grow before wood may be harvested in quantity, but you will be able to cut some withies within the first year. Willow withies and cuttings grow quickly and will give you a fine harvestable crop within two to three years, and the process may be repeated at regular intervals.*

45

What a load of rubbish!

Smallholders are the undisputed kings and queens of recycling and reuse. It's not because we're a parsimonious bunch; we just don't like to see anything wasted.

Smallholding makes creatives of us all. We are constantly using our problem-solving skills and our hands-on attitude, so it is unsurprising that we see everything that is thrown away as a missed opportunity.

Smallholders create a lot less waste to start with – we don't buy as many processed and packaged foods, for a start. What else we buy, we tend to reuse. We save any plastic bottles to cut in half and use as mini cloches, saving the tapered top half as hardy funnels for liquid manure. Wax fruit-juice cartons, with the lids cut off, can be used as moulds when making soap.

Glass bottles and jars may, of course, be saved for making home made cordials, flavoured vinegars, wines and ginger beer. Coloured glass mineral water bottles with screw tops are especially useful. Apart from cadging empty bottles from friends, restaurants may be glad to save them for you if you ask – it saves on their waste

Here's an idea for you... **Haunt reclamation yards for cheap and attractive materials for your garden. In small quantities, reclaimed engineering bricks, quarry tiles and even Victorian border edging can be bought for a pittance. Play around with them to make a pleasing and hardwearing design for paths. Add bottle ends, pebbles and cobbles for extra decoration. They can be laid on a bed of well-compacted rubble with a layer of mortar on top.**

removal bills. Similarly, glass jars are invaluable for bottling fruit, pickling vegetables and for chutneys, jams and jellies. Friends are happy to save their jars in return for a few refilled, jewel-coloured jars come autumn.

Newspaper is of great importance for the smallholder, and not just for keeping up with the news. It can be shredded and added to the compost heap (especially useful for a wet, whiffy heap that needs aeration). Newspaper can also be used as a weed-killing mulch, but be sure to weigh it down with stones. You can buy a cunning device for making 'logs' to burn on solid fuel fires (have a look in the stores on the Vegetarian Society website). It compresses newspapers into log-shaped bundles that burn slowly. As well as saving landfill (just like recycling paper) it also cuts your fuel bill.

From an environmental point of view, it is always worth saving water. If you are on a water meter, as many smallholdings and rural properties are, it also makes sense because you can save yourself money too. Make sure you buy water butts and water saving devices to attach to downpipes. You will be amazed by the amount of water saved by 'run off' and it will irrigate a huge amount of your vegetables. You can also fit cheap plastic guttering and downpipes to your greenhouses and polytunnels, together with water butts. The run off can save you having to haul water to your covered planting if it is some distance from the house.

Store water in cheap plastic drums, old baths or old loft tanks. Block off the pipe holes with mastic.

Find out how to make compost – the ultimate in recycling – in IDEA 39, *Magical muck*.

Try another idea...

You can also use 'grey water' (water used in the house) such as bathwater, for example. Fit a device to your downpipe from the bathroom to catch this water in a butt. Grey water can be treated in a specially purchased system, but if you use it straight away you will not encounter problems with small amounts. If you store grey water, it soon turns to 'black' water (stinky and slimy) and you wouldn't want it near your crops. I have used grey water effectively (we are on a meter) to water fruit trees and bushes, but I prefer not to use it on vegetables. Be aware that grey water can make a soil more alkaline, because of the chemicals added to bathing water, so don't use it on blueberry bushes or other acid loving plants.

Don't forget the old standbys for saving water too – install a dual flush toilet or put a brick in the cistern of an old toilet, and install spray taps. Don't leave the tap running as you wash your hands or brush your teeth.

While thinking of saving money on your utility bills, don't forget to turn off lights and appliances when they are not in use. And don't leave the TV on standby – overnight, it uses as much electricity as a night's viewing. That's bad for the environment *and* your pocket!

'We are a throw-away society. But there is no such place as "away". There is no such thing as "waste" in nature. Let's use nature's own design principle: zero waste.'
GRASSROOTS RECYCLING NETWORK

Defining idea...

199

How did it go?

Q **I'm having my windows replaced with double glazing to save energy. To save adding to the landfill crisis, is there anything I can use my old windows for?**

A *Old windows are a godsend for the downshifted gardener. I have several that I've used to make cold frames with – just make a simple box frame out of timber and attach the window on a couple of large hinges so you can raise the lid. If you have a quantity of windows, you can make a lean-to structure against a wall in the garden in a similar way, but this time making a deeper frame and fixing the windows directly to it.*

Q **I've had some trees and bushes delivered on pallets. Any ideas what I can do with the pallets when I've finished planting?**

A *I used four to make a quick compost bin. Basically, I nailed them together to make a lidless box and filled it with compost. You can also take them apart and used the wood to edge beds. Break up any planks that split and use them on your open fires.*

46

The Green Gym

Taking part in regular physical activity can halve your risk of developing heart disease. If gyms and sports centres don't appeal to you, consider your day-to-day activities.

Gardening and the general tasks you need to carry out as a downshifter get you moving and can have great benefits for your fitness levels and health.

The Green Gym movement was developed by the conservation charity British Trust for Conservation Volunteers (BTCV) and William Bird, a doctor from Oxford. A study of the first Green Gym in Oxford showed that regular activity improved members' cardiovascular fitness and their handgrip strength, which is a key to living independently for seniors. Those involved are also less at risk of osteoporosis (bone softening) and find their fitness levels rising.

Green Gyms encourage people to enjoy exercise, and the activities involve a range of practical conservation activities, such as forest management, fencing, hedge laying and building steps and walkways. These activities are, of course, also a boon to the environment and give participants a sense of pride.

Here's an idea for you...

Get together a working party of friends and relations to attack each other's gardens and plots together. Working in a group like this not only gets you fit – you carry on for longer because of the company – but the companionship and sense of a job shared is good for your mental health and sense of well-being too. You could map out a schedule to make sure everybody's plot gets a fair share of attention. This could turn into a gardening or downshifting group, where you all share information, seeds and tools.

You can enjoy the same benefits of the Green Gym by working on your own land. Digging, chopping wood, mucking out animals and cutting back undergrowth all increase cardiovascular activity and burn up lots of calories.

People who spend time outside gain many benefits. The negative ions in the air have a positive effect on people and refresh us. Salt crystal lamps are all very well, but a few hours in the outdoors will also lift your spirits as you reconnect with the natural world. Levels of serotonin (a neurotransmitter related to mood) have been found to rise when we are outdoors, so take advantage of working your land to increase your sense of well-being. A job completed well also gives you immense satisfaction – and improves your plot, so you win all round!

Digging gives you a great cardiovascular workout. Basically, it's hard work! Be sure to pace yourself and, weird as it sounds, it's worth warming up your muscles with a bit of stretching before you get stuck in. People pull muscles digging because they dive straight in, and you don't want to be one of them. Make sure you guard your back as you dig, too. Choose a spade that feels comfortable. If it is too short, and you are tall, you will hurt your back – so find a spade that has a longer handle, which you can use comfortably.

If you are small, think about using a border fork and spade. These are smaller, because they are made for working in small spaces, and they are not too heavy. I have used a set of these comfortably for years.

Want to find out about downshifted beauty techniques? Find recipes and tips in IDEA 47, *Clean, green beauty queen.*

Try another idea...

Cutting back undergrowth is also a great workout. Using a petrol strimmer with a brush cutter (my favourite mode of attack) uses up loads of energy as you balance the head of the tool and swing it gently backwards and forwards across the undergrowth.

Chopping wood raises quite a sweat. As the saying goes: it warms you twice – once in the chopping and once in the burning. If you have an open fire and/or a solid fuel stove, chopping wood will give you huge amounts of exercise. It's also a strangely rhythmic and soothing activity.

Fencing offers another heavy workout – moving the posts and wire, digging post holes, banging posts in. Having a smallholding is a sure fire way to increase muscle power! My muscle strength has increased greatly due to the regular workouts they get, and this increases your feelings of well-being and physical confidence.

Basically, instead of looking at exercise as a chore, to be scheduled and carried out indoors on specially designed machines, exercise becomes a part of your downshifted life. As you become less sedentary, your fitness levels will rise and your body will become healthier and more efficient. Welcome to the Green Gym! The dues are low and the benefits are enormous.

'A man's health can be judged by which he takes two at a time – pills or stairs.'
JOAN WELSH

Defining idea...

How did it go?

Q **The idea of a 'Green Gym' is all very well, but what happens in winter?**

A *Firstly, downshifting work doesn't grind to a halt because it's winter – some of the most active jobs, such as digging and chopping wood, are still needed on cold days. Secondly, according to a recent study from the University of Tennessee, exercising outdoors in the cold burns 12% more calories than the same workout indoors. This means you burn up to 32% more fat as your body works harder to keep warm.*

Q **How can working on the land make you as fit as gym work, which targets particular muscle groups as well as increasing your cardiovascular fitness?**

A *Easily! Most of the jobs you carry out on the land or in the garden as a downshifter raise your heart rate and thus give you a cardio workout. The key is that the exercise is regular for the downshifter. Unlike the gym, which you can decide to avoid for a few days, the work does not disappear on a smallholding. Animals still need feeding and mucking out; gardens still need to be kept watered and weed free. Conventional gyms are great, of course – as long as you go regularly.*

47

Clean, green beauty queen

**Cosmetics and toiletries are jaw-droppingly expensive –
for men and for women. So, take the downshifted option –
make your own!**

When you buy that expensive but oh-so-
pretty pot of cream, with all its beguiling
promises, you are paying for a dream wrapped up
in expensive advertising.

My mother always told me never to put anything on my skin that I wouldn't gladly
put in my mouth. It's good advice, and makes you smell quite deliciously edible.
The products we buy are cocktails of chemicals – even most of the products that
trumpet how 'natural' they are in their advertising. Parabens and phthalates, which
are potentially carcinogenic, are found in all manner of toiletries and cosmetics.
Phthalates are often found in hairspray, perfume, and facial moisturisers, and
parabens are present in many deodorants and toothpastes.

We absorb substances through our skin, so it makes sense to make those substances
as natural as possible.

Here's an idea for you...

Who needs expensive bath products? You can make your own bath bombs with materials bought cheaply from the chemists'. Mix together: 1/4 cup of baking soda, 1 tablespoon of ascorbic acid, 1 tablespoon of borax powder, and 2 tablespoons of icing sugar. Add 2 tablespoons of sweet almond oil, together with fragranced oil. You can also add herbs from your garden. Press the mixture firmly into moulds – cheap flexible rubber ice cube moulds are ideal. After a couple of hours these can be turned out onto waxed paper to dry for a few days. Store the 'bombs' in a closed container. To use them, drop them into your bath water and watch them fizz!

FACE

Honey, raw egg and oatmeal mixed together makes a lovely face mask (or a manly facial scrub). If you are having trouble with spots and blemishes, add a drop of tea tree oil for its antiseptic properties – but be cautious when using oils because they are very strong and can cause irritation if you use too much.

Kaolin powder or fuller's earth (types of clay) can be mixed with strong herb 'tea' or a couple of drops of soothing oil, such as chamomile, to make a pore-tightening face mask. Leave it on until it dries, then have fun scaring the cat and generally 'cracking your face' before you rinse it off with water.

Yoghurt – natural, not fruity and bitty – makes a good cleanser for all skin types, and jojoba oil (a type of liquid wax) makes a great moisturiser.

Make a gentle facial scrub by mixing ground almonds with rose water. You can make your own rose water by steeping rose petals in water in a jar on a sunny windowsill for a day or so (no longer or it will grow interesting fur; not something you would want to spread on your face!), and then adding a couple of drops of rose oil and a few fresh finely chopped petals.

HAIR

Find out how to grow the herbs to use in your potions in IDEA 48, *Home grown herbs.*

Try another idea...

Chamomile is well known as a rinse for bringing out highlights in blonde hair. Just make a strong 'tea' and use it as a last rinse after washing your hair. Rhubarb stems can be boiled and the liquor used to lighten hair. Wash your hair and comb through the liquid (made by boiling two sticks of chopped rhubarb in a pan of water until it turns to mush, then straining it). Leave it in for half an hour and then rinse.

Sage 'tea' can be used as a final rinse for dark hair, and 1 teaspoon of cider vinegar added to final rinsing water is good for making any shade of hair silky. Raw eggs, whisked in a jug, make a strange but effective conditioner for supple, shiny hair – just don't rinse with hot water or you'll end up covered in scrambled egg.

BODIES

Ground rock salt or sugar makes a wonderful and invigorating body and foot scrub. Add olive oil and a few drops of essential oil according to your mood, and even a few fresh chopped herb leaves such as mint or lemon verbena. Just scrub and rinse for baby soft skin!

BATHS

I'm tired of all this nonsense about beauty being only skin-deep. That's deep enough. What do you want, an adorable pancreas?
JEAN KERR, author and playwright

Defining idea...

Make a fragrant bath without getting bits stuck all over your body by simmering a handful of herbs or flowers in water for about 15 minutes. Leave the liquid to cool and sieve it before adding it to your bath. Alternatively, make mixtures of dried or fresh herbs and put them in small home-made drawstring muslin bags (Cut a circle of muslin and stitch round the edge – put the herbs in and pull the thread tight.) Hang them under the running bath water.

How did
it go?

Q   I'd like to make my own cosmetics because I'm against animal testing, but how can I be sure that the products I make are safe?

A   *Firstly, use the 'can I eat it?' test – that is, make toiletries from food substances. You can also do a patch test on your own skin. Rub a small amount of the cosmetic preparation you have made onto a small patch of your own skin and leave it overnight. The inner elbow is a good place because the skin is quite sensitive and it can be hidden if it goes blotchy! If all goes well and you do not have a reaction, go ahead and use your 'product'.*

Q   There are loads of ideas I'd like to try, but what can I store the goodies I make in?

A   *Well, you can reduce the amount of rubbish sent to the landfill site by reusing tubs and bottles you have bought, and friends save for you. I also buy pretty glass bottles and jars from junk shops. Make small quantities, and store your products in the fridge if possible, as they will last longer. Remember, cosmetic firms put preservatives into their products to make them last and you do not.*

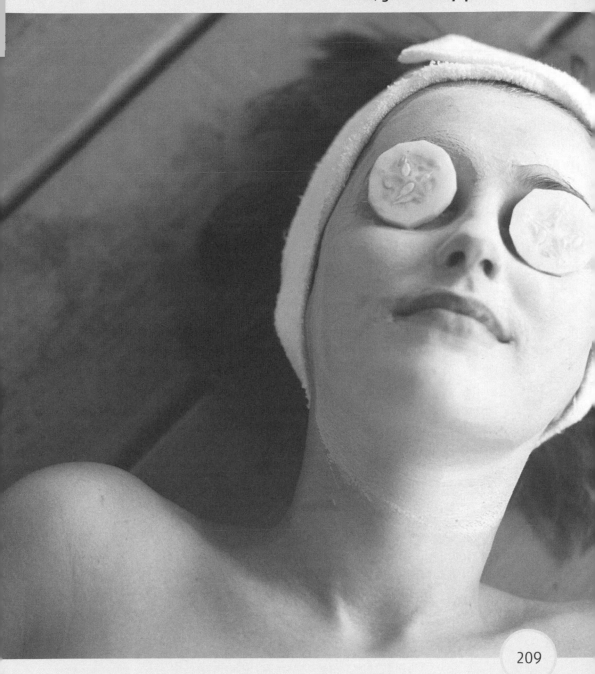

48

Home grown herbs

Herbs can be used to flavour food, make houses fragrant, dye cloth and 'doctor' animals – and humans! Every garden should have some.

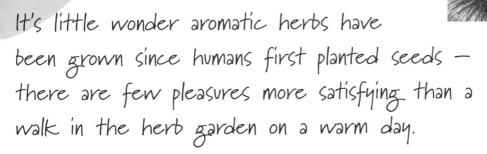

It's little wonder aromatic herbs have been grown since humans first planted seeds – there are few pleasures more satisfying than a walk in the herb garden on a warm day.

Besides the flavours and heady perfume, a herb garden also supplies you with a natural pharmacy. As with any self-administered remedy, though, take advice from a qualified practitioner as necessary.

Herbs generally like warmth and a sheltered spot. They also like well-drained soil, so prepare your soil by digging in plenty of grit to make it free draining (particularly if you are gardening on a heavy or clay soil).

There are perennial herbs – those that come back year after year – and annual herbs, which need sowing every year. Biennials are herbs that are sown one year and grow to maturity the next year before dying off and needing to be re-sown with new seeds. Read on to find out what you should grow, and why.

Here's an idea for you... **Make your own teas and tisanes. Use a small bunch of fresh herbs (about 25 g) or a heaped teaspoon of dried herbs, and put them in a small teapot kept especially for the purpose. Add boiling water and leave the herbs to steep. Strain them carefully to avoid getting 'salad teeth'. An old-fashioned tea strainer works well. Alternatively, you can buy a 'tea ball' – a small, spherical metal strainer on a chain – that you fill with herbs and dangle in a cup of hot water.**

PERENNIALS

Mint is the thug of the herb garden. Be careful about where you put it because you will never be rid of it. For this reason, many people like to grow it in containers. Bees and butterflies love this herb when it is in flower. Mint is a good culinary herb – lovely on tiny potatoes fresh from the garden – and makes a soothing tea, which is especially good for upset or unsettled stomachs and pregnancy sickness.

Rosemary bushes grow best in light soils, but having dug lots of grit into my heavy clay soil they grow prolifically here. Rosemary leaves, rubbed from a fresh sprig, make a fabulous flavouring for tiny roast potatoes and Mediterranean roast vegetables. In addition, rosemary makes a good astringent – just make strong tea and wipe the liquid across your skin to tighten pores. Rosemary also makes a rinse for putting glints and highlights into dark hair, and is good for dandruff sufferers.

Sage is a downy leaved plant that grows easily. However, it can become 'leggy', with long woody stems. Rather than cutting back hard, and potentially damaging the plant, I tend to take cuttings yearly. Sage is great for sauces and stuffings and the tea is also good for throat infections, or used cold as a mouthwash. Strong tea, used cold, soothes insect bites and stings.

Thyme grows easily on light soils, but heavy soils need grit dug in. Bees love the flowers in summer. Thyme is a great culinary herb, and is also a fine tonic for the digestive system – not just for humans but also livestock. Thyme tea with honey also promotes sound sleep.

If you want to sell your herbs, get some pointers by reading IDEA 51, *Farmers' markets*.

Try another idea...

ANNUALS AND BIENNIALS

Basil is a delicious culinary herb. It is perhaps grown best in containers inside to protect it from the weather. Apart from the green variety, you can now buy seeds of purple and ragged edged basil for variety. Home grown, organic basil makes the most wonderful pesto. Basil also has mild antiseptic properties.

Borage is a beautiful plant that I would not be without – not least of all because the flowers look so great in a jug of Pimms! They are also delightful when crystallized in sugar for dessert decorations. The tiny blue star-like flowers are irresistible to bees and other pollinating insects, so include a few borage plants in your fruit garden. It self-seeds easily, so once introduced will be there to stay.

Angelica is an architectural plant said to be an aid to fertility – so go steady! However, it also has culinary uses. The stem can be candied in sugar – it is the source of the tiny expensive pots of green sweetmeat sold by confectioners for decorating cakes and desserts.

Parsley is ubiquitous as a culinary herb, but also has great stomach soothing properties. Tea made from this plant will help to soothe cystitis. Chewing a sprig freshens spicy breath, too. Parsley is also good for livestock, and can increase milk yields.

'Like people, plants respond to extra attention.'
H. PETER LOEWER, plantsman

Defining idea...

213

How did
it go?

Q **I would like to dry some herbs for winter use. How should I go about it?**

A *Cut your herbs on a dry day and hang them in a dry place for two to three weeks. You can hang them on a nail or a special hanger, which can be bought or made by a local blacksmith. Once the herbs are dry, they can be crumbled and stored in airtight jars.*

Q **How do you candy angelica?**

A *Cut 6–8 cm pieces of stem and soak them in boiling salty water (10 g salt to 2 l of water) for ten minutes. Then put them in fresh boiling water for up to ten minutes, until tender. Scrape away the skin and immerse in sugar syrup, made by dissolving 175 g sugar in 300 ml of boiling water. Use this quantity for each half kilo of stem. Steep the stems for a day. Then drain the syrup, add 50 g more sugar and bring to the boil before pouring back over the stems. Do this daily for eight to ten days. Drain the syrup and lay the angelica on a baking sheet. Dry in a cool oven (100°F). It can then be stored in waxed paper in an airtight container.*

49

LETS make a difference

LETS is a system of local community-based mutual aid networks. It is ideal for downshifters who have limited financial resources.

People in LETS (local exchange trading system or scheme) barter goods and services with each another. There is no money involved!

The LETS movement started in Canada, but now extends around the world. A number of likeminded people form a group, putting together a list of the skills and goods wanted and offered by the members of the group. This list is sent out to members regularly, and the fun begins!

The knowledge and skills of the people who live in an area make up its real wealth. LETS keeps this wealth working in the community. People who have developed a wide range of skills and abilities are highly valued members of the LETS community – and these are people who may not have wealth or high-powered jobs in wider society. Elderly people, with a lifetime of knowledge and experience, are highly valuable to LETS groups. People who work full time caring for their children may have skills and experience that are poorly valued by society at large; however, their talents are recognised and further developed within the LETS community.

Here's an idea for you...

If you think you haven't got much to offer a LETS group, think again. Start by making a list of all the things you love doing. This may be massage, gardening, cooking, childcare, craft work, anything! Then look at the items cluttering up your house that you don't want or need and list them. Then make a list of the goods or services you'd like to have access to, but don't, because you can't afford them or can't justify spending money on them. Once you have your lists, you're ready to trade!

LETS groups can build members' self-esteem by empowering people and helping them to make their life more comfortable and debt free. Because they can get local goods and services through LETS, they spend less money and disposable income increases. LETS groups are different to conventional society, where the labours of some are valued more than others. Members set a value on their own labour and goods, and equality is maintained.

People feel less isolated if they are part of LETS. As part of an interdependent community, members have a reason to contact new people without 'cold calling', as it were. Elderly people, supporting parents, and single-income families with a stay-at-home parent can easily build new contacts and make friendships through a LETS introduction.

LETS members pay a small registration fee and are given a registration number. This number is needed for trading to begin. Members' lists of the goods and services they have to offer, and what they want to acquire, are published on a trading sheet. There is usually a charge (in LETS credits) per line for the listing – this pays the person who compiles the sheet. Regularly check your list to make sure it is up to date.

Many groups have regular meetings, which have a social aspect as well as an opportunity to trade. They tend to have a 'bring and share' meal, and trade goods, gardening equipment, plants and seeds as well as services. Groups also hold LETS

Project Days. These are days of activity as a group, organized to carry out a specific task. This can either be something for the benefit of your LETS group, such as setting up a website, producing literature or group promotion, or it can be for the benefit of an individual LETS member, perhaps someone moving house, renovating a house or a gardening project. All participants earn LETS points for their efforts.

Most groups elect a LETS Committee at an Annual General Meeting. These maintain LETS accounts and update trading sheets.

When a member finds someone offering a skill they need, or an item, they contact the person offering it and agree a price. The 'purchaser' pays for the service with a LETS cheque. Cheque books are issued to members and cheques are written out and given to the member who provides the goods or services. These are then sent to the group treasurer, who adjusts the members' accounts with debits or credits. The payments in your account may be used with any group member – it doesn't have to be a one-to-one trade between you and the person you traded with.

LETS is a great way to improve the quality of your life and the quality of the lives of others. The system rejects the consumerism that drives society today, where people are judged by what they have more than by what they do and are. And with LETS you can't get into consumer debt – part of what the downshifting ethos rejects. LETS also encourages you to become part of your community, which is crucial to becoming a successful and happy downshifter.

Want to escape consumerism? Read through IDEA 6, *Jump off the consumer carousel*, and step into a free life.

Try another idea...

'Money was invented so we could know exactly how much we owe.'
CULLEN HIGHTOWER, US salesman and writer

Defining idea...

217

Q   How can I find out more about LETS in my area?

A   There is an international LETS directory on the website LETS-Linkup.com. It has links to many other sites with information on LETS groups. Ask at your local Citizens Advice Bureau and local council too. If there isn't one convenient for you, think about starting your own!

Q   I'd like to start a group and have found the information I need to get going, but I'm worried that I won't be able to attract enough new members to make the group viable. Do you have any suggestions?

A   Put notices in the 'What's On' section of the local newspapers (often free) and think about running a LETS stall at street festivals, fairs and markets. Give out flyers at garden shows and community events. Don't forget the power of word-of-mouth publicity. Telling friends and family about your latest LETS 'bargain' is probably the best way to spread the word.

50

Boxes of delights: brown box organic schemes

Many people today order organic vegetables to be delivered on a regular basis via 'brown box' schemes. As a smallholder, you may wish to join a scheme as a supplier.

Organic food is no longer considered 'alternative', nor is it only to be found in health food shops. Organically produced food is a growing mainstream consumer trend.

Whether it is disquiet about food production as a result of the BSE crisis, GM food and animal welfare, sales of organically produced food are growing quickly. The annual market share has risen to over a billion pounds in the United Kingdom alone. Many farmers are converting to organic methods as they become economically viable. We should not forget that intensive farming methods were a response by farmers pushed into over-production to make a living, using herbicides, pesticides and fungicides to produce as many crops as possible from their land.

Organic is a legally defined term. There are very strict guidelines to adhere to if you wish to become certified as an organic producer. These are laid down by both

Here's an idea for you... **If you want to learn about growing with organic principles, join the Henry Doubleday Research Association or similar organic group near you. (Check out hdra.org.uk/links/index.php for worldwide information.) The HDRA has a scheme called the Heritage Seed Library (and other organisations have similar schemes). This is a system that organises the growing, saving and distribution of heritage seeds that are no longer available for sale. You can become a seed guardian and grow seeds, especially to save them for distribution.**

national and international laws. It is an offence to use the word unless a product has been certified by a recognised organic agency. In the United Kingdom, The Soil Association certifies up to 70% of organic food produced.

Farms gain organic status by going through a two-year conversion period, during which no chemical fertiliser or pesticides may be used. Once the farm is certified as organic, the farmer does not use such chemicals at all.

Food produced with less than 70% organic ingredients is not legally allowed to use the word *organic* on its label. If you are converting to organic status, your labels are permitted to say 'under conversion to organic farming'.

Organic produce does seem to go 'off' sooner than other food, but that is down to the lack of artificial preservatives. The food does taste better, though! Organic food can be more expensive, but many community organisations are able to give you information about bulk-buy schemes that can make things more affordable. Brown box schemes can be a cheaper way to buy organic food because it comes straight from the supplier to you, cutting out the middle-man.

To join an organic box scheme as a consumer, you pay a fixed amount to receive a regular (sometimes weekly) box of organically produced fruit and vegetables. The produce available varies with the seasons, and vegetables may include carrots, potatoes, cabbage, sweet corn, kale, chard and salad vegetables amongst others. The fruit on offer includes strawberries, raspberries, grapes, apples and pears. Some box schemes e-mail customers with a list of what is ready to pick, so you can order what you want to be delivered. The food is fresh, and you are supporting local producers. Some suppliers will also deliver meat, wine, dairy produce and dry goods.

Search online for lists of these box schemes to find one that you think will best suit your needs.

BECOMING A SUPPLIER

Brown box schemes are mushrooming (sic) wherever there are organic growers. In Victoria, British Columbia, several brown box programmes deliver by bicycles fitted with specially designed aluminium trailers – and that's about as green as you can get.

If you would like to become a brown box scheme supplier, first you must apply for certification as an organic holding. This takes time. There are many certification bodies, such as The Soil Association. Your first step is to contact the organisation and request an initial

Thinking about going self-employed as you downshift? IDEA 10, *Getting down to business*, will give you a head start.

Try another idea...

*'Manifest plainness
Embrace simplicity
Reduce selfishness
Have few desires.'*
LAO TZU

Defining idea...

221

application form. Once this is filled in and submitted, the certifying body will arrange to send an inspector for an initial visit, after which he or she prepares a report for the certification committee. If your application is approved, a certificate is issued. Organic registration and certification requires a licence fee.

You must keep detailed records of your food production processes if you wish to be certified as an organic producer. You will also be subject to annual and random inspections to make sure you adhere to organic production guidelines at all times.

How did it go?

Q   Surely pesticides are safe; they've been used for so many years. What's all the worry about?

A   *Pesticide residues are found in many foods. Over four hundred chemicals are licensed for use in farming, and nobody really knows the long-term effect of these chemicals on the human body. Links have been made between some pesticides and illnesses such as cancer. If you can reduce your intake of these chemicals, it would seem to make sense to do so.*

Q   Where can I find out more about organic gardening?

A   *There are some good books available. Try* **The Organic Kitchen Garden** *by Juliet Roberts (Conran Octopus, ISBN 1-8409-1394-0), the* **HDRA Encyclopaedia of Organic Gardening**, *edited by Anna Kruger (Dorling Kindersley, ISBN 1-4053-0891-5) or Bob Flowerdew's* **Organic Bible** *(Kyle Kathie Ltd, ISBN 1-85626-595-1).*

51

Farmers' markets

Farmers' markets have sprung up all over the world, in urban areas as much as in the country. They are ideal outlets for your surplus produce.

The farmers' markets offer consumers superb quality, fresh, often organic food, cutting out the middle-man and bringing people — even in the city — to the 'farm gate'.

When the public goes to farmers' markets, they can buy products direct from farmers, growers or producers from a defined local area. This may be fruit, vegetables, dairy products, fish, meat or game; it may also be cooked goods such as preserves and baked goods. Only produce that has been grown, brewed, farmed, smoked, baked, preserved or created by the stallholder may be sold.

Farmers' markets are wonderful for consumers – the general public – because they are able to ask questions about the products they are buying face to face with the producer. If it is important to you, you can ask if any meat bought has been produced ethically and how the animals have been reared. A farmers' market can help to educate consumers about the origin of all their food, and they can be a great source of ideas on how to cook fresh and possibly unusual ingredients.

Here's an idea for you... **If there's not already a farmers' market in your area, consider starting one. To get ideas on how to do this, contact your national association of farmers' markets (e.g. farmersmarkets.net in the UK). You will need to assess whether there is a demand, and find a good site. You will also need to set a budget. Remember that for a market to be sustainable, stall fees need to cover insurance and promotion.**

They are also great for producers – particularly small producers, such as smallholders. The markets offer a low-cost entry point to selling for many farmers and smaller producers who have perhaps not sold directly to the public before. If you downshift to a smallholding and want to sell your produce, the local farmers' market may well be the way to go. There are many markets, and producers may now have stalls at a variety of different markets. This is good even for larger scale farmers who are looking for diversification ideas and can use farmers' markets to sell their specialised products. Farmers' markets have made a huge difference for some farmers and have meant the difference between bankruptcy and survival.

Because farmers' markets remove the middle-man and allow direct selling by producers, profits are higher. They have the added benefit for sellers of providing regular cash flow, with a regular outlet, which can be crucial for new producers, such as a smallholder, who may well have organically produced goods to sell. (Note that you mustn't label goods as 'organic' unless you have official certification – label it 'produced without pesticides'.)

Farmers' markets also help to regenerate town centres. Retailers report higher sales on days when farmers' markets are held and people are attracted to the area. This can have a knock on effect for employment and local prosperity. Farmers' markets can also promote dialogue between rural and urban communities, which is crucial at a time when rural life is under threat as schools and amenities (such as post offices, etc.) close and unemployment rises.

If you're considering not just growing but supplying food, check out IDEA 50, *Boxes of delights: brown box organic schemes.*

Try another idea...

Studies have recently found that many schoolchildren are unable to name fruit and vegetable types and are unaware of how they are grown and produced. Exposure to farmers' market produce will help to rectify this.

SELLING ON THE WEB

In these days of mass web connectivity, the internet should be ignored as a selling opportunity – at your peril! Big Barn (www. Bigbarn.co.uk) is a virtual farmers' market that connects local food producers to consumers. Producers can register their business and advertise their produce for a small fee. Consumers register and are sent details of producers in their local area. The site also offers delicious local and seasonal recipes designed to offer consumers ideas on how to prepare fresh produce. How do you fancy Cabbie Claw, Cullen Skink, or Dublin Coddle?

In addition, the site offers a variety of interesting articles on food production. Oh yes, and look out for Carrotman. He's a superhero for the locally produced food community. Honestly.

The FARMA (National Farmers' Retail and Markets Association) website offers consumers a list of food producers in their local area.

'I can get up in the morning and look myself in the mirror and my family can look at me too and that's all that matters.'
LANCE ARMSTRONG

Defining idea...

A similar point of contact in the USA is ams.usda.gov/farmersmarkets/. For information on European farmers' markets check out thefoodpaper.com and in Australia and Canada follow the links at hydroponics.com.au. Basically, wherever you are in the world, there is a farmers' market near you!

How did it go?

Q   Farmers' markets seem a more 'green' way of shopping. Is this just image and smokescreen or is there any basis in fact for this viewpoint?

A   The 'green' image of farmers' markets isn't just about hessian and twine wrapping! Firstly, environmentally aware farming practices, such as organic and pesticide-free production, are encouraged. They also encourage farm diversification – and, therefore, bio-diversity. Farmers' markets also help reduce 'food miles', as products are brought to the market by local producers; they are not flown in or hauled hundreds of miles by lorry. Vehicle pollution is therefore reduced along with traffic noise and the use of fossil fuels. There also tends to be less packaging on food sold at farmers' markets.

Q   Do I need a licence to sell goods at a farmers' market?

A   No, but your production may be subject to inspection. You have to be a bona fide local food producer, and you or your representative who is directly involved in producing the food has to sell it. You have to fulfil environmental health regulations if you offer cooked goods, which are quite stringent in terms of hygiene and cleanliness.

52

Downshifting to another country

A restaurant in Spain or a guesthouse in Greece? Downshifting to warmer climes may be your ultimate dream, but it could go sour if you don't plan the move properly.

Think carefully about what problems you could face in not just changing your lifestyle, but changing countries too.

People downshift to other countries for a variety of reasons. They may want to experience a different lifestyle, perhaps having had a taster while on holiday. Property may well be cheaper, offering the chance of a more relaxed lifestyle.

For many years, Spain has been a retirement destination for northern Europeans. More recently growing numbers of people are moving there to live and work, perhaps to less highly paid, but less stressful jobs.

Before you take the plunge, however, it is well worth taking a long hard look at the area you wish to move to, and your own motivation. Do your homework and you are much less likely to find yourself on the next plane home, sadder but wiser.

Here's an idea for you... **Language teachers are in demand, so consider taking a course to teach your native tongue to your hosts. Teaching English as a foreign language (TEFL) is one such course. Then advertise. Even notices in shop windows can bear fruit. Work can then be done to supplement your income, even if you are planning to grow your own food.**

PROPERTY

With property prices continuing to rise sharply, buying an affordable family home with a decent garden can seem like an impossible dream for many young people wanting to settle and have children. Going on holiday has allowed people to see the standard of living and the cost of housing in other countries. It often seems so much cheaper, and the way of life can feel much more relaxed. Of course, it would do, to you … you're on holiday!

Search around on property websites and specialist magazines to get a handle on the cost of property in the area you favour. It helps to have an idea of what you can expect for your money before you start looking seriously through agents.

Make sure you can afford to take holidays to your target areas to check out the services available. It can be very isolating moving to a new country, especially if you are not fluent in the language, so make sure you know how and where to seek information to make your projected move as smooth as possible. Are there any extremes of weather conditions? How hot does it really get? What's it like in winter – many areas surrounding resorts can bubble with activity in summer but a lot might shut down out of season. Once you start viewing properties, make sure you see your potential new home in winter or bad weather as well as on a hot summer's day.

LANGUAGE

It goes without saying that you need to learn the language of the country you have chosen – otherwise you will miss out on many aspects of life, including companionship. Children will learn quickly to communicate – perhaps because they are less self-conscious as well as being more linguistically adaptable. It can actually be more difficult to make sure they retain their native tongue, especially as they are totally immersed in the foreign language at school.

Help yourself by learning the basics of the language at least before you go. Sign up for evening classes. Watch and listen to the appropriate satellite TV channels and radio stations. Watch your DVDs in the appropriate language (you have many options with modern DVDs) with subtitles in your native language at first.

Once you get to your destination, listen and interact as much as possible. The local market and shops are great places for meeting and talking with people. You learn a lot by jumping in at the deep end!

Worried whether the family might jinx your ambitions? You should be. Find out why in IDEA 3, *All aboard?*

Try another idea...

'Live as if you were to die tomorrow. Learn as if you were to live for ever.'
MAHATMA GANDHI

Defining idea...

WORK

Be very clear about what you will be able to do to earn money. Make sure you know what permits or licences are needed before you can work or run a business, as well as the tax and insurance benefits you can expect. If you are working for yourself, the same applies. Be sure to do your homework before you depart to save extra stress when you arrive. It's amazing to watch TV programmes about people with no catering experience who decide to buy a bar abroad and then can't understand why it doesn't work out.

Similarly, if you are intending to live self-sufficiently, make sure you research what will and will not grow on your new property. Remember, orange or olive groves look idyllic but they are arid places – so, if you are not prepared to spend time and money on irrigation, your garden may well not be very productive.

Q   **When we went to Portugal on holiday, the cost of living was much lower than here. Would we be able to save lots of money if we moved there?**

How did it go?

A   *Possibly, but although relocation for a cheaper lifestyle may work in the long term, it won't in the initial stages. Initial set-up costs abroad are expensive, and the complications that may arise can cause anything but relaxation. Research is the key to minimising the financial hassles you face.*

Q   **We have children and are thinking of downshifting abroad. Apart from the obvious language adaptation needed, what else should we consider?**

A   *You need to do a great deal of research into the schooling system of the country of your choice – unless, of course, you can take up the home schooling option. Moving countries with younger children is probably easier than with teenagers. Youngsters may find it easier to adapt whereas it can be harder for teenagers to integrate successfully and their schooling might suffer.*

The end...

Or is it a new beginning?

We hope that the ideas in this book will have inspired you to try new things, given you an insight into what downshifting is really all about and encouraged you to escape from the pressures of the 9 to 5. How far you choose to scale it down is now up to you.

So, why not let *us* know how you got on? What did it for you – what helped you reach for your hoe, buy some chickens or start growing your own organic produce? Maybe you've got some tips of your own that you'd like to share. If you liked this book you may find we have more brilliant ideas for other areas that could help change your life for the better. You'll find us, and a host of other brilliant ideas, online at www.infideas.com.

If you prefer to write, then send your letters to:
Downshift to the good life
The Infinite Ideas Company Limited,
36 St. Giles, Oxford OX1 3LD, UK.

We want to know what you think because we're all working on making our lives better too. Give us your feedback and you could win a copy of another *52 Brilliant Ideas* book of your choice. Or maybe get a crack at writing your own.

Good luck. Be brilliant.

Offer one

CASH IN YOUR IDEAS

We hope you enjoy this book. We hope it inspires, amuses, educates and entertains you. But we don't assume that you're a novice, or that this is the first book that you've bought on the subject. You've got ideas of your own. Maybe our author has missed an idea that you use successfully. If so, why not send it to yourauthormissedatrick@infideas.com, and if we like it we'll post it on our bulletin board. Better still, if your idea makes it into print we'll send you four books of your choice or the cash equivalent. You'll be fully credited so that everyone knows you've had another Brilliant Idea.

Offer two

HOW COULD YOU REFUSE?

Amazing discounts on bulk quantities of Infinite Ideas books are available to corporations, professional associations and other organisations.

For details call us on:
+44 (0)1865 514888
Fax: +44 (0)1865 514777
or e-mail: info@infideas.com

Brilliant resources

Fieldcraft and Farmyard Ground for Beginners, Valerie Porter, Swan Hill Press (1-85310-164-8).

Storey's Basic Country Skills: A practical guide to self-reliance, John and Martha Storey, Storey Publishing (1-580172-62-4).

The Survival Handbook: Self sufficiency for everyone, Michael Allaby, Macmillian.

The Good Life, Sally Gordon, Book Club Associates, London.

The Complete Book of Self-sufficiency, John Seymour, Faber and Faber (0-5711-1095-9).

Out of Your Towny Mind: The reality behind the dream of country living, Richard Craze, White Ladder Press (0-95439-144-6).

Downshifting: The Ultimate Handbook, Andy Bull, Thorsons, an imprint of HarperCollins Publishers.

Choosing Simplicity, Linda Breen Pierce, Gallagher Press (0-96720-671-5).

The Simple Living Guide, Janet Luhrs, Broadway (0-55306-796-6).

Women Rule the Plot, Peter King, Duckworth (0-7156-2949-2).

The Complete Urban Gardener: Growing your own fruit and vegetables in town, David Wickers, Book Club Associates, London.

Gardening With Cloches, Louis N. Flawn, Garden Book Club.

Practical Country Living, Guy N. Smith, Boydell Press (0-8511-5495-6).

Gardening Under Plastic: How to use fleece, films, cloches and polytunnels, Bernard Salt, Batsford Ltd (0-7134-8448-9).

Exploring Country Crafts, J. Geraint Jenkins, EP Publishing Limited (0-7158-0469-3).

Practically in the Country, Patrick Humphrey and Tom Gabriel, Comma International Biological Systems (0-95139-770-2).

Country Wines and Cordials, Marshall Cavendish Editions (0-8568-5856-0).

Build Your Own Buildings, Frank Henderson, Dairy Farm Farmers (Books) Limited, Lloyds Chambers, Ipswich.

Home Doctoring of Animals, Harold Leeney, Farm and Stock Breeder.

The Smallholding Plan, compiled by *Country Garden and Smallholding Magazine*, Broad Leys Breeder Company (0-90613-724-1).

Handy Farm Devices and How To Make Them, Rolfe Cobleigh, The Lyon Press (1-5582-1432-1).

Home Farm: A practical guide to the good life, Paul Heiney, Dorling Kindersley (0-7513-0461-1).

Good Husbandry, H. I. Moore (now out of print but grab a copy if you see one in a second-hand bookshop).

Where it's at...